Service Learning in the Middle School:
Building a Culture of Service

Service Learning in the Middle School:
Building a Culture of Service

by

Carl I. Fertman

George P. White

Louis J. White

National Middle School Association
Westerville, Ohio

National Middle School Association
4151 Executive Parkway, Suite 300
Westerville, Ohio 43081
1-800-528-NMSA
NMSA **www.nmsa.org**

Printed in the United States of America
ISBN: 1-56090-108-X   NMSA Stock Number: 1232

Second printing February 2002

Library of Congress Cataloging-in-Publication Data

Fertman, Carl I., date.

Service learning in the middle school: building a culture of service/by Carl I. Fertman, George P. White, Louis J. White.

        p.   cm

Includes bibliographical references (p.).
ISBN: 1-56090-108-X   (pbk.)

1. Student service--United States. 2. Student volunteers in social service--United States. 3. Middle school students--United States. 4. Community and school--United States. 5. Curriculum planning--United States. 6. Experiential learning--United States.
I. White, George P., date. II. White, Louis J., date. III. Title.

LC220.5.F47   1996
361.3'7--dc20   96-15861

Table of Contents

Special Introduction

S ervice learning connects young people to the community. Students learn what the problems are, who is working to solve them, and how to help out. This important attachment enables young people to be positive contributors. The constructive activities of service learning, identifying and solving community problems such as illiteracy, health hazards posed by smoking, and the loneliness of the elderly help young people avoid the pitfalls of early adolescence — drugs, gangs, pregnancy.

In Maryland, we have a service learning graduation requirement. We feel so strongly that students have something to offer that we formally engage them. In several Maryland school districts middle schoolers participate in activities such as those described in this book to fulfill that graduation requirement. During the six years I was at the Maryland Student Service Alliance we found over and over again that middle schoolers have energy, idealism, and seriousness of purpose to serve effectively. We also found that service learning enhances and supports other reform efforts such as cooperative learning, performance instruction and assessment, and interdisciplinary curriculum.

This volume provides wonderful, insightful guidance to teachers and administrators launching service learning initiatives and to those wanting to enhance an existing program. The ideas here will stimulate you to design service learning programs that meet the special needs of your students and community. Creating and sustaining a service culture in middle schools will, ultimately, serve us all.

— Kathleen Kennedy Townsend
Lieutenant Governor
Maryland

Foreword

Americans of all ages have always identified strongly with the underdog. Young adolescents, especially, become genuinely concerned about the less fortunate and readily commit themselves to projects that address such a need. Is there a middle school that hasn't sponsored a can-a-thon, Thanksgiving baskets for the needy, or a campaign to save an endangered species?

While one-shot service activities are common, neither tying them into the ongoing curriculum nor using service as a means of fulfilling academic and developmental objectives of middle level programs has occurred, except in scattered instances. A strong and certain wave of the future in education, however, is the inclusion of service activities into the school program with accompanying expansion of school/community relationships. So many of the accepted objectives of middle level schools cannot easily and readily be met within the school itself or through traditional classroom instruction; but these often vague, yet critical objectives can be met very effectively and efficiently as students engage in planned and supervised service activities.

As young adolescents mature they seek to engage in experiences that have inherent worth and importance. Schoolwork, which all too often seems artificial, loses much of its appeal to these rapidly growing young people with their new-found curiosity, broadened interests, and intellectual prowess. Unable because of their age to seek regular employment, they are good candidates for engaging in service learning projects that give them the opportunity to participate in activities that have validity, even if not yielding financial rewards.

Incorporating aspects of service into the ongoing academic program is a wise move, since it benefits not only the agency receiving service but also the school and its students. The service learning movement is not just an educational fad. It is a solid, not-to-be-denied trend in American education. All middle level educators should become knowledgeable about and active in promoting service learning.

This volume is comprehensive, specific, and replete with examples and guidelines. It can be used by any school seeking to enhance the achievement and total development of its students. In addition to ample discussions of all aspects of service learning, this resource includes an extensive listing, with full addresses and phone numbers, of organizations and groups that are involved in some phase of service learning. This resource should be available to and used by every middle level school that truly seeks to provide the best possible education for its students.

— John H. Lounsbury

CHAPTER 1

Building a Culture of Service at the Middle Level

Middle schools provide a particularly favorable environment in which to create a culture of service that truly links service and learning. Such a culture of service evolves from the middle school philosophy that promotes teachers and students working together to meet the educational and developmental needs of students. A culture of service can be especially strong here because middle schools promote experimentation, risk-taking, collegiality, and cooperation among administrators, teachers, and students.

Service activities already exist in most middle schools. Through participation in car washes, bake sales, dances, read-a-thons, walk-a-thons, and 5K races, middle school staff and students have traditionally raised money for many groups and organizations engaged in combating health and social problems. Toy drives and food collections give hope to the hungry and bring happiness to many needy children. While some students and teachers raise money and collect food and toys, others provide thousands of hours of more direct service. They work at hospitals, provide support at the Special Olympics, clean parks, assist at shelters and food banks, tutor other students, staff hotlines, and visit the elderly. Young people and their teachers can also be found speaking at public hearings, serving on policy boards, and visiting elected officials to talk about the needs of the community. Outside of school, students and teachers are involved in many community organizations, such as Boys and Girls Clubs, Volunteer Fire Fighters, 4H clubs, Future Farmers, and Boy and Girl Scouts. Religious organizations also teach the value of service through their many programs. These organizations and others involve young people in service activities.

1

Similarly, if you walk into any middle school you will hear and see teachers and young people in the process of learning. In science, students learn about life science, which includes the study of the human body and ecological systems. In math, students learn to estimate, measure, and apply problem-solving skills to real life situations. In English and language arts, they develop communication skills and expand their reading interests. In social studies, the content spans U.S. history and world cultures. In art, students develop an understanding and appreciation for art and explore their own artistic and creative abilities by experimenting with different art media. In music, students develop an understanding and appreciation for music and explore their own musical talents. Health focuses on drug and alcohol awareness and human growth and development, particularly in relation to students' own bodies, physical fitness, and development of a healthy life-style. Technical education includes computer application skills as well as traditional industrial arts areas such as woodworking, electricity, and ceramics. In home management or home economics, students learn nutritional and family life skills and are educated about child development and care. Learning is certainly what middle schools are all about.

When learning activities and community service activities become linked, we have the beginnings of the desired culture of service. The process of linking service and learning is *service learning*. It is built upon existing community service traditions, activities, programs, and initiatives and springs from ongoing collaborations between schools and communities. Bridges are built between the academic program and the community. The community becomes an extended classroom where students apply their knowledge and practice their skills. Service learning builds a culture of service that promotes student participation in solving community problems. It also enhances learning and helps to develop a sense of caring and responsibility.

Service learning can be defined as an instructional methodology whereby young people can be involved in real life settings in which they can apply academic knowledge and previous experiences to meet real community needs as a regular part of the curriculum (ASLER, 1993). The service learning process involves preparation, service, reflection, and celebration. Although it is related to both community service and volunteerism with which middle schools have long been involved, service learning is unique in that it links community service and volunteerism with academic learning (see Figure 1). This means that it is not an add-on to existing programs within a school, but instead is a methodology that infuses service into the school's curriculum. Service is the learning activity. It is also a collaborative effort that brings schools, community-based organizations, parents, and other citizens together in a common enterprise of individual and community growth (Fertman, 1994).

Service learning connects students to the community, placing them in challenging situations where they associate with adults and gain experience and knowledge that can strengthen and extend their school studies. Service learning helps to make classroom study relevant, since young people discover connections between their actions and the world that exists beyond the school's walls and the content they study in the curriculum.

Most middle school students have few opportunities to associate with adults outside of their school and home. As discussed in *A Matter of Time* (Carnegie Corporation, 1992), too many children are raising each other with little stabilizing assistance from adults. The isolation young people often feel has resulted in a rift between them and society's institutions. Service learning is beneficial because it involves youth in active roles in the community and establishes new relationships between young people and an adult facilitator; hence, it can be a powerful force in closing that rift. Furthermore, it dramatically alters the roles of middle school students in both the school and community. Youth become resources, problem solvers, and producers of goods and services rather than passive, consuming members of the community.

Figure 2 highlights some of the major role changes experienced by students as a result of service learning.

Figure 1
What is Service Learning?

Service learning is a method by which young people learn and develop through active participation in thoughtfully organized service experiences ...

- that meet community needs;
- that are coordinated in collaboration with the school and community;
- that are integrated into each young person's academic curriculum;
- that provide structured time for a young person to think, talk, and write about what he/she did and saw during the actual service activity;
- that provide young people with opportunities to use newly acquired academic skills and knowledge in real life situations in their own communities;
- that enhance what is taught in the school by extending student learning beyond the classroom;
- that help foster a sense of caring for others.

(from Alliance for Service Learning in Education Reform, 1993)

Figure 2
Changing Roles of Youth

In the traditional view youth are:	In service learning youth are:
users of resources	resources
passive observers	active learners
consumers of service	producers of service
in need of help	helpers
recipients	givers
characterized by a feeling of helplessness	leaders in social change

Because of the roles they realize through service learning, young adolescents feel more connected to their communities. They find that they can make a difference in the environment and in their lives. This is crucial in a time when alienation and isolation have unfortunately become the norm for a significant portion of our youth.

The foundations of service learning

Service learning is not a new concept. It is based on a number of existing linkages between schools and communities and is grounded in three closely related philosophical foundations: 1) the writings of John Dewey; 2) experiential education; and 3) citizenship education.

Dewey viewed education as process-oriented and child-centered. For him, teaching was not focused on presenting subject matter to prepare students for some set of future conditions, but rather on using a child's existing experiences as a springboard for further learning. Dewey (1916) defined education as the "continuous reconstruction of experience." He believed that young people want to encounter and gain control over their environment. In confronting their world, they run into problems, and it is in dealing with these social problems that young people bring forth their intelligence and past experiences.

Experiential education, which is closely related to progressive education, views education as the continuous reconstruction of experience. It contends that students learn through interaction with their environment and through the effective use of experience. Simply put, it is learning by doing. But it is not just "doing." Experiential education places emphasis on reflecting upon experience in an attempt to determine what it is that is being learned. This processing of the information one learned is the foundation for the service learning concept of reflection (Newmann, 1989).

Those in the citizenship education movement assert that education is an essential aspect of democracy. Its focus is on developing values that are consistent with democratic living. In today's society, few people are actively engaged in democratic institutions. Service learning, therefore,

can be viewed as a powerful strategy to reunite democracy and education (Barber, 1994).

In the last decade we have viewed the growing interest in service
learning as an opportunity for educational reform. Research findings
suggest that service learning can be a powerful tool for putting learning
in context, engaging alienated youth, introducing problem solving into
schools, providing career exploration opportunities, and strengthening
school/community relations. A series of recent studies and reports from
High School (Boyer, 1983) to *Turning Points* (Carnegie Corporation,
1989), and *The Forgotten Half* (W.T. Grant Foundation, 1988) have recommended service as a strategy for youth development. Service learning is supported by national organizations like Campus Compact, with
its 418 colleges, the National Youth Leadership Council, the National
Society for Experiential Education, the Constitutional Rights Foundation, and Youth Service America. The concept has spread rapidly and
has been incorporated into the educational policies of many states, including California, Colorado, Maryland, Minnesota, and Pennsylvania.
Maryland has even made seventy-five hours of community service a
statewide high school graduation requirement.

Service and the curriculum

Service learning redefines service as an activity undertaken to produce learning. It is shaped by the curriculum, or it can even *shape* the
curriculum. Teachers and students create and complete service activities to achieve specific learning outcomes. Therein lies the salient difference between service learning on the one hand, and volunteerism
and general community service on the other. Community service and
volunteerism may be, and often are, powerful experiences for middle
school students, but volunteerism and community service become service learning when there is a *deliberate* connection made between the
service and the learning that is accompanied by conscious reflection on
the experience.

Shaping service to fit into the curriculum is more than a matter of matching students to a task needed by a particular agency or community organization. It should not be an isolated activity performed by students that is unrelated to life in the school. In some schools, service activities have unfortunately been perceived as required. This is not service learning. Rather, service learning builds a culture of service in middle schools by weaving service into the fabric of the school. Service and learning become intertwined in an ongoing process that is connected to larger community needs, with students contributing in multiple ways across the curriculum throughout the year. Service, therefore, is viewed neither as an isolated entity nor as just a high school requirement for graduation.

The community problems addressed through service learning are real, and the students contribute their energy and knowledge to meet those needs. Partnerships that involve sharing of resources develop between the school and community groups, individuals, and organizations. For instance, students supply the labor to build community playgrounds, the town provides the land, community groups purchase individual pieces of playground equipment, a local contractor prepares the land, and a local architect develops the plan. In each step and with each group, students are a part of the process. In addition to the learning and hands-on experience, students gain an understanding of themselves as partners in solving community problems. Furthermore, service learning empowers local community members to be community problem solvers.

In building a culture of service at the middle level, the potential for activities is unlimited. Figure 3 lists potential service activities and sites, some within schools and others in the community. It should be understood that service within one school can, and often does, extend to other schools to become a district- or community-wide project.

Figure 3
Potential Service Activities

Within Schools	*In the Communities*
Tutoring fellow students	Health programs
Mentoring younger students	Senior companions
Cross-age education	Literacy programs
Working with physically & mentally challenged students	Working with physically & mentally challenged adults
Conflict mediation	Hunger awareness programs
Peer counseling	Creek reclamation
New student orientation	Park restoration
Hunger awareness	Homeless shelter adoption
Drug and alcohol awareness programs	Community history projects
School improvement projects	Animal adoption programs
Parent council projects	Supporting cultural institutions

Learning outcomes for service learning are consistent with those established by most middle schools. Conrad and Hedin (1989) detailed service learning outcomes for students, schools, and communities (Figure 4). Service learning provides opportunities to meet the following goals:

- intellectual development
- basic skills development
- moral and ethical development
- social and civic responsibility
- career preparation
- multicultural understanding
- personal growth

Figure 4
Service Learning Outcomes

STUDENT

Personal Growth and Development
- Self-esteem
- Personal efficacy and sense of responsibility
- Moral development and reinforced values and beliefs
- Exploration of new roles, identities, and interests
- Willingness to take risks and accept new challenges

Intellectual Development and Academic Learning
- Basic skills, including expression of ideas, reading, and calculating
- Higher level of thinking skills, such as problem solving and critical thinking
- Skills and issues specific to service experience
- Motivation to learn
- Learning skills, including observation, inquiry, and application of knowledge
- Insight, judgment, and understanding

Social Growth and Development
- Social responsibility and concern for others
- Political efficacy
- Civic participation
- Knowledge and exploration of service-related careers
- Understanding and appreciation of, and ability to relate to, people from a wide range of backgrounds and life situations

SCHOOL
- Paradigm shift – teachers as coaches and facilitators; students responsible for their own learning
- Motivated learners engaged in authentic and significant work
- Cooperative learning environment

- Teachers as reflective practitioners engaged in planning, curriculum development, and inquiry
- Collaborative decision making among administrators, teachers, parents, students, and community members
- Positive, healthy, and caring school climate
- Community involvement, resources, and support in the educational process

COMMUNITY

- Valuable service to meet direct human, educational, health, and environmental needs
- Schools as resources – school/teacher/student teams serving as researchers and resources in problem solving and community development
- Empowerment – school/community partnerships to assess, plan, and meet needs collaboratively
- Citizenship – students become active stakeholders in the community
- Infusion of innovation toward improving the institutional practices of schools and communities
- Understanding and appreciation of diversity – across generations, cultures, perspectives, and abilities

Source: Conrad and Hedin, 1989

To establish effective service learning, two prerequisite conditions must exist: the school must create a vision that perceives service as a way to educate the student as a whole person, and the local community must view the school as a potential resource to help assess and address community needs and opportunities. Once both conditions are in place, there is very little limit to the possibilities that might emerge from service learning.

To guide schools and communities as they develop service learning, a number of groups have joined together to produce principles of practice. These include the National Society for Experiential Education (Honnet & Poulson, 1989) and the Association for Service Learning and Educational Reform (ASLER, 1993). It is important to become familiar with these principles before initiating a service learning program.

Service learning:

1. Provides concrete opportunities for youth to learn new skills, think critically, and test new roles in an environment that encourages risk-taking and rewards competence.

2. Encourages students to perform service that makes a contribution to the community, addresses local concerns, and prevents future problems. (In this context, the school may also be defined as the community.)

3. Constitutes an integral element in the life of a school and in the surrounding community.

4. Involves preparation, reflection, and celebration as essential elements.

5. Involves youth in planning from the earliest stages.

These principles are guideposts for thinking about service learning. There are, however, many ways to achieve a culture of service. It can start in the community or the school, with a club, a special event, or a single teacher using a service activity as a part of a unit. It is not a fixed concept that can only be implemented one way. Rather, it is an evolving concept that has many possibilities, a process that can be and is utilized by educators and community professionals whenever they engage youth in service. The distinction of service learning as a process and not just a product is important. A teacher does not wake up one Monday morning and decide to install service learning in his/her classroom. Rather, service learning is practiced when service is used by a teacher to enhance learning and to reaffirm a culture of service.

Service learning and the middle level learner

In recent years service learning has expanded rapidly in middle schools. One reason for this is the publication of *Turning Points*

(Carnegie Corporation, 1989). The report provided an impetus for the development of service programs across the country.

One methodology that *Turning Points* recommended was connecting schools with their communities by identifying service opportunities in the community, establishing partnerships and collaborations to ensure students' access to health and safety services, and using community resources to enrich instructional programs. Although many schools were already involved in community service, this recommendation encouraged many other middle school staffs to develop and support service learning.

However, the value of service learning must also be calculated in terms of how the service experience fits the needs and characteristics of the learners. The true value of service learning can only be appreciated when it is viewed within the framework of the world of middle school students. An understanding of students ages 10-15 reveals tremendous diversity in their development, maturity levels, behavior, and understanding of the world and of themselves (National Middle School Association, 1995). Young adolescents need opportunities to behave responsibly, to demonstrate their growing capacity for self-control and self-management; to explore aptitudes, interests, and special talents; to broaden their awareness of the world; and to develop accurate and positive self-concepts (National Association of Secondary School Principals, 1985; National Middle School Association, 1995).

Stated simply, students benefit both as individuals and learners when their educational experiences reflect their developmental characteristics. It is, therefore, important that a thorough understanding of the unique characteristics of young adolescents serve as the basis for developing a culture of service. Figure 5 identifies some of the more common needs of 10-15 year olds that must be taken into consideration. Service learning provides teachers with opportunities to create an environment where these needs are met. By starting with the needs of the students, the teacher is able to select and design experiences that meet middle school students at their developmental level.

Service learning is attractive to middle level learners because it appeals to their idealism and their quest for independence. The idealism of young adolescents comes from their emerging ability to think about their expanded world and their capability for developing many possible responses to social situations that are not tempered by actual experience. They have notions of ideal families, ideal schools, ideal religious institutions, and ideal societies, and may rebel against the imperfect ones they experience. Young adolescents cannot understand why the rest of the world does not accept their idealistic solutions to social, economic, or sociological problems (Muuss, 1980). They may become angry and express unwillingness to accept reality, or as is frequently the case, they ally themselves with the underdog and those they see as less fortunate. Although this behavior is sometimes frustrating to adults who must deal with their passion, Menge (1982) pointed out that "active imagination and the dreaming of ideals are not wasteful activities ... but can be a constructive part of everyone's life, making for the improvement of human functioning in a socially meaningful way" (p. 419).

Developing a culture of service and providing frequent opportunities for students to apply what they are learning to real world situations provides them with a creative and useful vehicle for recognizing that they can make a difference. A curriculum that integrates service lets students "test" their solutions to the problems facing them and allows them to develop a modified sense of idealism – an idealism grounded in the reality of what is and what is possible.

The quest for independence and autonomy plays a powerful role during early adolescence. The emergence of self-understanding and self-reflection allows young people to begin differentiating themselves from their parents and teachers while still maintaining an awareness of their dependence. This duality can create internal and external conflicts. The individual expends considerable energy trying to gain greater control over his or her life and increased freedom from authority, while at the same time trying to hold on to the perks of childhood (Thornburg, 1983). Juhasz (1982) noted that it is during this stage of development that individuals begin to seek identities that are separate from their parents and to try to somehow make a difference in a wider social perspective.

Figure 5
Some Needs of the Young Adolescent

1. **Understanding the physical and emotional changes** that occur during puberty. These changes are personal and frequently become troublesome matters. The child needs help in understanding himself/herself during this period of change and accepting the idea that it is healthy to grow and evolve.

2. **Self-acceptance.** Resolving the conflict between what one is and what one wishes to be. Beginning to establish life goals and making reasonable plans to attain those goals.

3. **Acceptance of and by others.** Developing acceptable relationships with peers of both sexes. Making friends. Getting to know others and understanding their differences. Realizing how one affects others. Understanding the dynamics of peer pressure.

4. **Acceptance,** understanding, approval, and love from significant adults.

5. **Learning responsibility** to others. Not completely self-centered. Learning self-control.

6. **Learning to make decisions,** assuming responsibility, using independent judgment, recognizing and facing the consequences of one's actions.

7. **Learning to deal with feelings.** Becoming aware that others experience similar feelings.

8. **Developing a personal value system.**

Service learning programs can help meet students' needs for independence; they give them the opportunity to assume leadership roles as they identify, coordinate, and complete projects that have real significance. As a school or individual teacher embarks on a campaign to create a culture of service, it is crucial that students be provided with opportunities to have their voices heard. Students must see themselves and their projects as independent from their parents and, to an extent, from their teachers if the value of service is to become internalized.

Early adolescence is a crucial period for identity formation. Answering questions like Who am I? and How do I fit into the world? are defining tasks for the 10-15 year old. It is during this stage of development that individuals begin to establish and clarify a social consciousness and start to learn socially responsible behavior (Havighurst, 1972; Kohlberg & Hersh, 1977). Erikson (1980) indicated that during pre-adolescence (10-12 years of age) individuals define themselves by what they can do and by the skills they possess. As students progress (12-15 years of age), they begin to clarify their role in their world (the school and local community) and define and refine their unique identities. Students look for qualities they admire in role models and heroes and try to integrate those ideals into their own value systems (George & Alexander, 1993).

The society of the school and beyond becomes immensely important to young adolescents, and teachers become crucial agents in fostering a sense of competence. Middle level schools with well-integrated values of service support healthy experimentation of skill application, provide opportunities for students to interact with individuals and groups that have views of the world that differ from their own, and develop students' ability to reflect on who they are, what they do, and the impact of their actions.

This publication explains how to connect schools with communities to meet the needs of middle level students by incorporating service learning and building a culture of service. Δ

Service Learning, Curriculum, and Teams

W hy is a middle school a likely environment in which to build a culture of service? Clearly, the basic tenets of the middle school concept support the creation of a culture of service through service learning wherein the needs of young adolescents will be well served.

The middle school movement continues to expand, with most middle schools conscientiously trying to work "for the student." Many have adopted slogans and mission statements that claim that "kids come first." School administrators make a special effort to hire staff who can deal with the diversity that characterizes 10-15 year olds, who are flexible, and who are able to adapt programs to meet the needs of students. Rules are not applied arbitrarily, procedures are consciously designed to be less confusing, and interdisciplinary teams work to create integrated learning activities. Middle level teachers also know that their students question everything, can be very issue-oriented, and exhibit eagerness to "do something about these problems."

Many schools became middle schools because the community realized that the way junior high schools traditionally operated was no longer appropriate for today's young adolescents. Too many junior highs were simply junior versions of high schools. Nowhere was this more apparent than in the curriculum, where the content of every subject seemed to be a simplified, watered-down version of high school subjects and often contained information that was duplicated at the higher level. Thus, many junior high students complained that what they were doing really didn't count, and this encouraged them to delay "getting serious" about studying until they reached high school.

As the middle school movement has encouraged honest analysis of school programs, it has become apparent that a content-only curriculum is insufficient as a means of meeting the needs of young adolescents. The sheer volume of information available to teachers, especially in social studies and science classes, has made it impossible to "get it all in." At the same time, students regularly tell us that soon after the test they forget what they have been "taught." Thus most students "play school," regurgitating enough right answers to get a grade, knowing all along that they probably won't use the information later.

Recognition of this weakness in public education has led to reforms that ask the key question all educators must answer. What should students know and be able to do when they leave school?

When faculties are asked to answer this question, they typically focus on certain basic areas: Are students leaving us able to read, write, and speak intelligently? Do they know and can they apply basic math skills? Will they be responsible citizens? Relatively few staff members talk about the *content* of their subject. Yet, when they are asked to compare what they currently do with what the goal they know they should pursue, there is little relation between the two.

It is becoming obvious to more and more educators and citizens in general that we must help youngsters become lifelong learners, because in their lifetime that is the single most important skill they will need. They will probably face up to five lifetime career changes and therefore will need to be adaptable in many work situations. This skill will be far more important than the often changing and largely irrelevant content of many courses.

Curiously, most staff members understand this perfectly well and blame state- or district-driven curriculum requirements for their inability to adopt more skill-based programs. However, as more school districts adopt curriculum reforms that focus on broad outcomes and assessment programs that address the application of skills and knowledge, the time seems ripe for infusing more lifelong skills into the curriculum.

In *A Middle School Curriculum: From Rhetoric to Reality* (1993), James Beane proposes a middle school curriculum based on the educational interests and concerns of adolescents. This would obviously require the teacher to include class members in curriculum planning before beginning to teach. It is fairly easy to predict what students will identify as personal concerns: their own developmental changes, finding a place in their peer group, their future, questions of values and attitudes, and how to deal with adults.

Likewise, when asked to identify societal concerns locally and beyond, students typically speak of the interdependence of the world's people, today's environmental concerns, issues arising from cultural diversity, and the fast pace of technology and its potential effects on society.

Beane (1993) points out that these are really not two different lists, but rather two very similar ones, which differ only in degree. Thus, the adolescent's desire to find a place among his/her peers is a microcosm of what happens among the nations of the world. Beane then goes on to suggest how a middle school curriculum might be built around such themes as "interdependence," "justice," or "conflict resolution," thus reflecting these concerns.

Each theme provides a vehicle and a means for achieving appropriate knowledge. More importantly, a theme also provides a vehicle for teaching and using skills related to community, problem solving, computing, and research. In focusing on the theme, students will develop their self-concepts, take social action, and engage in critical and reflective thinking.

According to Beane (1992), the curriculum should have the following characteristics:

1. The curriculum at the middle grades should be grounded in the questions and concerns of the adolescent.

2. The primary use of knowledge ought to be to help early adolescents search for answers to questions they and the world have.

3. Neither knowledge nor skills are ends in themselves. Both need to be pursued in a context in which their use is apparent and real.

4. Adolescents and their teachers need to have more control over the specifics of their educational programs.

5. Curricula should have less to do with content-based "performance" objectives and more to do with posing and clarifying personal and social questions.

6 It is possible and even likely that as a result of using such a curriculum, different students will learn different things.

7. The curriculum needs to be constructivist – that is, it needs to enable young people to construct their own meanings rather than simply accept those of others.

8. Rather than emphasize the affective or the academic, the curriculum must focus on connecting these two areas.

What does all of this have to do with service learning? Implementation of service learning can help the middle school meet virtually all of the curriculum goals outlined above. Adolescents do not need to be coaxed into performing service. They are aware that their community has social and environmental needs, and many are eager to tackle them. If students are given some choice in a service project, they will have a real investment in their learning. In preparation for actual service, they will learn about the issues surrounding the need for their project's completion, whether it be environmental information related to park refurbishment, or social information related to the elderly. Since it is necessary that students learn about these issues prior to performing service, the teacher has an opportunity to present appropriate cognitive information.

Service provides authentic and hands-on experiences. Kids are given an opportunity to dig in and perform important tasks with their hands as well as their minds. Along with the knowledge that is gained from studying the issues related to service, many skills identified by staff as being vital can be taught not only in the classroom but also in a real life context. Written and oral communication will certainly be important, but so will problem solving, computing, and research. And while performing service, how could students not learn important lessons about civic responsibility and the need to take social action, to say nothing of critical and creative thinking?

As stated earlier, middle level curricular reform models share many of the same characteristics as those proposed for effective service learning. However, service learning provides a structured method to achieve those outcomes in the following ways.

1. Students are able to address their concerns and questions because they are allowed to choose the service activity they will work in.

2. Rather than acquiring knowledge in isolation, students will see knowledge applied.

3. Skills will be applied for a specific purpose and not learned for their own sake.

4. Because the entire team will help decide how to perform the activity, they will have some control over that portion of the curriculum.

5. Rather than evaluate learning by a test, service activities can be evaluated authentically. Was the service completed as predicted? Were tasks performed by students effectively?

6. Participants will have different experiences and learn different things from performing service. The reflection phase of this process helps students to consider what they have learned. What did it mean to them to work on the service activity?

7. Both affective and cognitive curriculum goals are realized.

Service learning enables students to learn how to be learners; it makes the student the *worker* and the teacher the *coach*. Most of all, it helps make school "real." The service learning process, therefore, is congruent with the goals and tenets of the middle school concept. It supports and extends the middle school model. However, the reasons to use service learning do not stop here but go beyond to the middle level team.

The middle level team and service learning

Teaming is the organizational heart and soul of an effective middle school. Service learning expands the team concept to include members of the community, and it serves to involve students more actively in the team.

Effective teams typically spend common planning time on two types of issues: one is the academic and general welfare of their students, and the other is the educational program for the team. The program is typically interdisciplinary, and instruction focuses on a central theme to which the major disciplines relate, rather than focusing on individual subjects separately. Thus, a team may adopt the theme of "change" and then teachers in various disciplines suggest ways they might contribute to the study of the theme. It is readily apparent how science, social studies, math, reading, and English can all contribute to such a theme.

The theme selected provides the eventual focus of a service activity. For instance, a team that chooses to beautify a nearby park might select "civic responsibility" as its theme, while a team that is teaching computer skills to senior citizens might choose "intergenerational communication."

In either case, this theme becomes the hub of the curricular wheel, as illustrated in Figure 6. The next step is to decide how the various subject areas can relate to that theme. It is not necessary for all disciplines to relate equally to the theme. Environmental issues will elicit many contributions from science, while social ones will generate more from social studies. It is important to involve students in identifying the topics to be pursued, possible activities, and the ways in which each subject can contribute.

Figure 7 illustrates contributions made by a group of students to the theme of civic responsibility.

The next step is to compose questions that will direct the study and make it meaningful. These questions help to organize the contributions of team members and become the table of contents for the unit. For example, guiding questions for this theme might include:

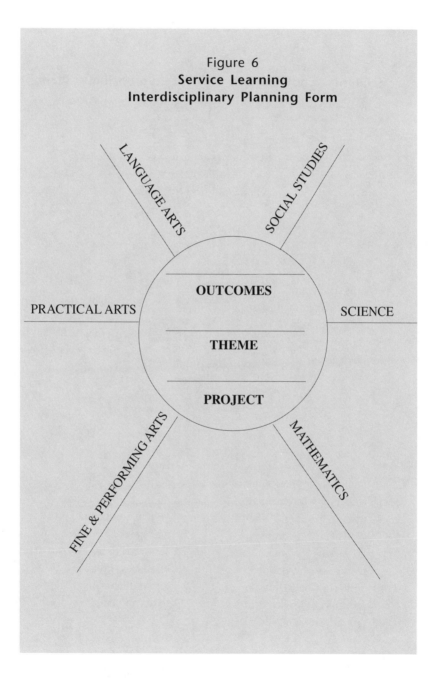

Figure 6
Service Learning
Interdisciplinary Planning Form

Figure 7
Students' Contributions to Civic Responsibility Plan

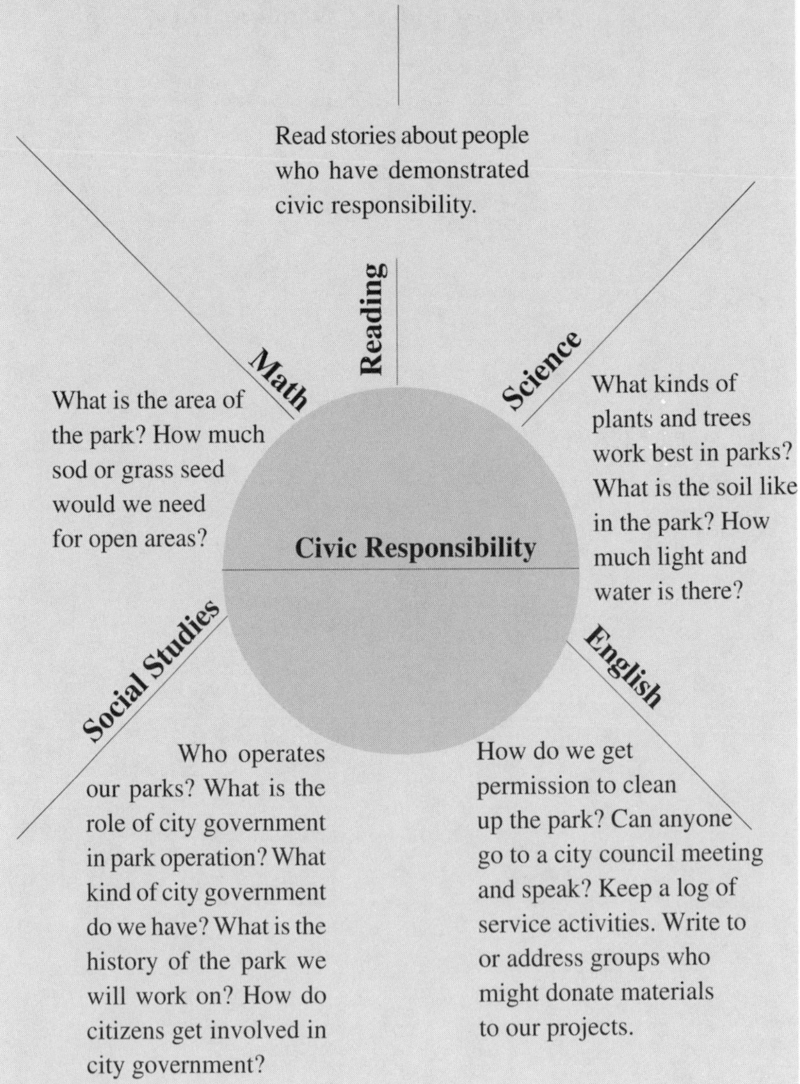

Read stories about people
who have demonstrated
civic responsibility.

Reading

Math

Science

What is the area of
the park? How much
sod or grass seed
would we need
for open areas?

Civic Responsibility

What kinds of
plants and trees
work best in parks?
What is the soil like
in the park? How
much light and
water is there?

Social Studies

English

Who operates
our parks? What is the
role of city government
in park operation? What
kind of city government
do we have? What is the
history of the park we
will work on? How do
citizens get involved in
city government?

How do we get
permission to clean
up the park? Can anyone
go to a city council meeting
and speak? Keep a log of
service activities. Write to
or address groups who
might donate materials
to our projects.

1. What is civic responsibility?

2. How have citizens in American communities demonstrated civic responsibility?

3. What happens when civic responsibility is ignored?

4. How can our team demonstrate civic responsibility?

Once the guiding questions have been identified, the means of carrying them out can be determined. Certainly, the implementation of the service project will be one of these activities, but others may need to precede this step.

Integrating service with all subjects may not initially be possible in every school. Service projects can be integrated with one or two subjects. One school has linked a very successful community lead detection program with its health classes, while in another, Tech Ed students designed and produced toy trucks, manufacturing enough of them to distribute one to every youngster in a nearby children's home. In still another school, all eighth grade science students were involved in creating a natural habitat in one of the school's courtyards as a part of that grade's science curriculum.

Once service learning is initiated in one subject, it is natural for an interested language arts teacher who has the same students to link much of his or her content to the service initiated through another subject. Thus essays and journals written in English class can become reflective pieces on service learning experiences, rather than entries about artificially created situations. Many service learning projects start either with environmental issues, which can then be linked to science, or social issues, which can then be linked to social studies. When all the students involved in these projects are on the same team, the language arts teacher on the team has many opportunities to use the service to provide authentic application of many of the skills he or she would otherwise teach in isolation. By recording oral histories, conducting interviews, giving presentations before various audiences, and corresponding with government and business officials, students can improve their communication skills.

Even if a school cannot initially form a complete team that focuses on service learning, it can start with an interested staff member who initiates a single project. Once the project is underway, other teachers who have the same students will see ways to extend coursework in their subjects to include the service learning activity, making instruction in their classroom more functional. Δ

CHAPTER 3

Elements of Service Learning

The linking of learning and service distinguishes service learning from general community service and volunteerism. Service learning is a teaching strategy with wide application across the curriculum. The four major elements of service learning are *preparation, service, reflection,* and *celebration* (Figure 8).

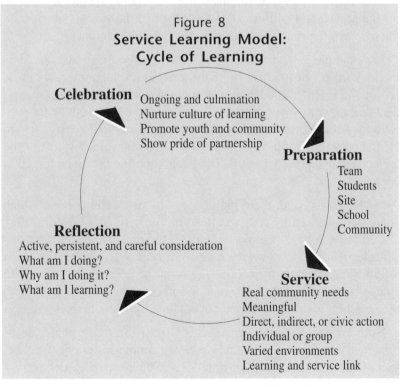

Figure 8
Service Learning Model:
Cycle of Learning

Celebration
Ongoing and culmination
Nurture culture of learning
Promote youth and community
Show pride of partnership

Preparation
Team
Students
Site
School
Community

Reflection
Active, persistent, and careful consideration
What am I doing?
Why am I doing it?
What am I learning?

Service
Real community needs
Meaningful
Direct, indirect, or civic action
Individual or group
Varied environments
Learning and service link

Preparation

Preparation focuses on linking service learning activities to the on-going, existing curriculum and to specific learning outcomes. In addition, it is during the preparation stage that students begin to learn how to function in the "classroom" of service.

Linking service learning activities to specific learning outcomes can take place in two ways. One is to start with a particular service focus and work toward a specific learning outcome; the other is to start with a specific learning outcome and work to develop a related activity.

In the first, a grade level or team service learning theme is established to act as a guiding focus in organizing and shaping the group's activities. The theme can be very specific, such as fighting illiteracy, or more general, such as helping the homeless. The theme provides scope for the project and helps to keep the efforts of the various subjects on track. Next, the team develops specific learning outcomes.

For example, if the project's goal is to refurbish a city park, students might learn about the history of the park in social studies, about its ecology in science, and about its dimensions in math. In English, students could write to vendors explaining the project and asking for supplies for park refurbishment, while in art, students could design a logo for the park renewal project. Sometimes certain subjects won't fit the theme, and that is okay as well. The integration should not be forced or contrived.

On the other hand, there may be an existing learning topic which could be enhanced by a service learning project. In a unit on "How Government Works," teams could adapt the park project to have students learn about their own town's government. While in the process of refurbishing the park, they learn who is on the town council, who is in charge of the parks, where the money comes from, and how to write to or speak before the town council in conjunction with the park project.

Both strategies transform teachers from the traditional role of imparters of information to a new role as learning facilitator. Teachers focus increasingly on preparing students to be lifelong learners.

Another purpose of the preparation element is for students to develop a clear sense of what the project hopes to accomplish and what they themselves can learn from each service learning activity. Topics that should be addressed in preparing for each activity include: how to perform the actual service work, information on the individuals who will be served, information on the social and contextual issues related to the service, information about the the service site, and problem solving when difficult situations arise. Group building exercises among participants should also be conducted before, during, or even after the service activities. Students should be actively involved from the start in deciding a site, selecting what team members and the agency are each expected to do, and planning for recruiting, training, supervision, and evaluation. Students should also help plan for reflection on the experience.

The preparation element helps to change the nature of the interaction between the school and community. The goal is to build organizational commitment and create a support system for the culture of service and service learning. To achieve this goal there must be participation by more than the individual members of the team; the process must involve the entire school and community. Chapters 4, 5, 6, and 7 discuss in detail building commitment and a support system.

As part of the preparation phase, teachers activate a service support system in the community. For example, the teachers and students might identify potential service sites. These sites can either be located within the school or in the community. Once the specific sites and learning objectives are identified, site personnel will prepare to work with the students. Likewise, the service support system within the school is activated. This includes communicating about the activity with administrators and parents. Administrative requirements are also addressed in the preparation phase. Initially, the details of preparation may seem overwhelming. However, as the service support system develops, preparation becomes the shared responsibility of students, school, families, and community.

Service

The second element of service learning is performing the actual service activity. It involves spending time with, attending to, and caring for others. Adults and students are active participants in the service activity. Observation is not enough; service needs to be hands-on.

In the process of designing the activity, the following questions aid in exploring possible connections with different units of instruction.

1. Could students teach what they have learned (skills or knowledge) to others? Examples are reading or computer skills.

2. Could the results of the students' efforts be contributed or presented to someone? Examples are cleaning up a city park or adopting a room at a shelter for abused women.

3. Could the classroom learning be applied to the service or used to find a solution to a real problem in the school or the community? Examples are staging a hunger banquet followed by a school-wide food collection.

The service must fulfill two needs. First, it should be challenging, engaging, and meaningful for students. Second, the service must address a real community need so that students perceive both the activity and their participation as relevant and important. They must believe that what they are doing makes a difference.

This process is further enhanced when students play a significant role in designing the service experience. The more the students are involved, the greater their sense of ownership will be, and therefore their investment in the program will be greater. Student service learning activities generally fall into three main categories: direct service, indirect service, and civic action.

Direct service. Direct service is defined by personal contact with individuals in need. Of the three types of service, students often find this type the most rewarding because of the direct contact with those they are helping and the immediate positive reinforcement they received. One example of a direct service project is participation by middle school students in reading with elementary special education students. Whatever the task, it is advantageous for students to be involved over a period of weeks or, preferably, months to that they can develop relationships with those they are serving, to gain a deeper understanding of the problem they are working on, and feel that they are making a significant and lasting contribution.

Indirect service. Indirect service is easy to organize because it involves channeling resources to solve a problem, rather than direct involvement with the individuals in need. Fund raising and food collections are examples of indirect service. Students support an organization's service or efforts to meet a community need but do not have regular contact with the individuals receiving the services.

Civic action. The third type of service learning activity is civic action, which emphasizes active participation in democratic citizenship. It usually includes two main activities: informing the public of the nature of the problem to be addressed, and working toward alleviating that problem. Students may petition the local government for better housing for the homeless, or they may initiate a consciousness-raising campaign to focus public awareness on the problem of student drug and alcohol abuse. When students are committed to a particular cause, they can be very effective in bringing about political change.

In a middle school, it may be appropriate to organize projects sequentially. Students are first involved with civic action, followed by indirect and then direct service. The time and duration of each activity are determined by the learning objectives and other circumstances. For example, students might be involved with an ongoing project, such as a stream restoration, over the course of a term; or their involvement might be limited to a few hours of service as part of a community health fair. Likewise, service can be an intensive multi-week experience. An example is a school that during the last three weeks of the school year involved all its students in a service learning activity in the community. Activities can also take place over the summer vacation or during school holidays. Furthermore, as service learning grows, schools begin to think developmentally. Year to year sequences develop. New projects and opportunities spring from previous efforts, new community needs are identified, and new curriculum areas infuse service into their coursework. The key is to always link the service activity to learning.

Shaping the experience for students also involves considering whether the service should be performed by an individual or a group. Middle school students may be reluctant to work on a project alone, but will participate willingly with a partner or a group. Students may be assigned in pairs to different sites, performing distinct but related tasks, or they may serve at a variety of sites completing the same individual project or task. One example of the latter type of service is an oral history project in which students are placed at homes for the elderly or visit shut-ins. Frequently, a number of students serve at the same site, performing individual tasks. Service activities with hospitals typically follow this format.

Group service activities are structured to promote team building and cooperation among participants. House rehabilitation projects, community clean-ups, volunteer fire fighting, and recreational projects are frequently cited as examples where teams of students work together to provide a needed community service.

A powerful factor in a service activity is the environment in which it takes place. Service activities take on additional energy and provide more learning for participants when they place youth in environments that are physically, culturally, socially, or economically different from their own. Although the impact will vary, working in another school building, a different section of the city, or a rural or urban setting seems to make a difference in terms of what participants gain from an activity.

A final factor to consider is the difference that it makes to share the service learning experience with another age group. Intergenerational programs are often undertaken with older citizens partnered with youth on a service activity. Some states also sponsor service corps programs, in which individuals seventeen or older and want to participate in one or two years of service activities, either full- or part-time, are given monthly living stipends and receive a post-service educational benefit that is applicable for college tuition.

Reflection

The third element of service learning is reflection, which serves to strengthen both the service and learning components. Reflection is essential in service learning and is viewed along with curriculum infusion as a feature that distinguishes service learning from volunteerism and community service activities. Reflection involves active, persistent, and careful consideration by students of their service activity, behavior, practices, effectiveness, and accomplishments (Fertman, 1994). Reflection means asking basic questions of oneself, such as: What am I doing? Why am I doing it? What am I learning? It helps students understand the meaning and impact of their efforts and allows them to link what they have learned with what they have done. Without reflection, students would probably just go through the motions of service, cognitively unaffected by the experience, with their personal ignorance and biases either reinforced or unexamined.

Reflection is also a means of assessing one's own behavior and satisfaction. It differs from traditional evaluation since its emphasis is on assessing oneself. Reflection can and often does include traditional evaluations of student performance, paper-and-pencil tests, written reports, and oral presentations. However, it also provides an opportunity to do such activities as maintain a journal, conduct a small group discussion, and perform individual projects. Reflection can include students speaking and writing about their service. Multimedia presentations can be put together. An activity that demonstrates and shares the service experience can also be a reflection vehicle. Figure 9 shows a model for generating reflection that was adapted from the National Youth Leadership Council (1991) and incorporates speaking and writing activities and multimedia presentations.

Reflection is thinking. However, it is more than simply bringing something to mind, encouraging students to carefully consider what they think. During a period of reflection, students can meditate, muse, contemplate, ponder, deliberate, cogitate, reason, and speculate. The goal of this phase is to achieve higher levels of thinking.

Figure 9
Generating Reflection

SPEAKING

- one-on-one conferences with teacher leader
- whole class discussion
- small group discussion
- oral reports to group
- discussions with community members or experts
- talks on project – for parents, school board, etc.
- teach younger students
- testimony before policy makers

WRITING

- essay, research paper
- journal or log – daily, weekly, or at conclusion
- case study, history
- special project report
- narrative for a video or slide show
- guide for future participants
- self-evaluation or evaluation of program
- newspaper or magazine articles
- portfolio

GENERATING REFLECTION

How do we help students develop new understanding, skills, and knowledge from service learning?

ACTIVITIES

- gather information on a project
- workshop presentations
- surveys or field-based research
- simulation or role playing
- plan training session for others
- celebration programs
- plan future projects
- recruit peers to serve
- plan budget

MULTIMEDIA

- photo illustrated or slide essay
- video documentary
- painting, drawing, collage, etc.
- dance, music, or theater presentations

Reflection is the framework in which students process and synthesize the information and ideas they gain through their service and in the classroom. During the process of reflection, students analyze concepts, evaluate experiences, and form opinions – all in the context of the school curricula.

Practicing reflection helps young people gain a greater sense of themselves. For example, when learners are asked to think about their own goals and progress in a service learning activity, they have the opportunity to master self-assessment skills, which can help them to become more independent learners. They acquire insights, which allow them to build on their strengths and to set goals in areas where they know they need further development. Reflection also offers teachers an opportunity to identify the special new knowledge that students gain through service.

Many of the outcomes claimed for service learning depend on a regularly scheduled reflection component. Although the experience provides a rich source of information and generates thoughts and feelings for students to learn from, interpretating these data increases their ultimate impact. The job of reflection is to provide a thoughtful context in which students can make enlightened sense of their experiences. It is a task that prevents reinforcement of preconceived biases and opens the door to real learning and often to significant change. Done well and done often, reflection can become a lifelong habit that contributes to greater self-assessment and critical awareness for individuals.

There is no single form that is superior to others, and using varied forms may be beneficial in order to appeal to a larger number of participants. Reflection activities should be planned during the stage of preparation. The advisory period also provides an excellent time for reflection. While there are many equally effective forms of reflection (Toole and Toole, 1995), several fundamental elements are present in all quality reflections.

First, reflection is structured; it has a clear objective. Second, the method selected is consistent with the desired learning outcome; for example, directed writing activities based on the service performed foster directed learning. Journal writing fosters personal growth, and small group discussions are often effective in promoting group building. Third, all students are involved in reflection and in linking the experience to their lives. Fourth, students are helped in assessing what they have learned and judging their own progress. Finally, reflection is ongoing. It occurs throughout service learning, not just at the end of an activity.

Reflection as an engaging, ongoing process is interactive and interesting – a two-way street to be integrated throughout the service experience. One of the ways to make reflection relevant to students is to maximize the number of connections it has to the curriculum. Using academic material to improve service and applying lessons learned in field activities to academic material ought to be an interactive process. A variety of methods can be used to capture all the possibile benefits of students' experiences and to match these to their ways of learning.

Celebration

Celebration is about sharing across and among systems, organizations, and individuals involved in service learning. Students celebrate learning and achievement. They are recognized for their demonstration of learning in real life situations that address community needs. Students share in large and small ways with their community, families, and peers what has been gained and given through service. The variety and forms of student celebrations are numerous.

Ongoing celebrations recognize incremental learning and involvement. Noting the number of service hours on report cards, highlighting information on service projects in school newspapers, flyers sent home to parents, holding pizza parties, and listing students' names and service projects on school and community-based organizations' bulletin boards are examples of ways to recognize and celebrate student service. These same postings are often found in the community as well. For example, poster displays of service activities can be mounted at post offices, local restaurants, real estate and insurance offices, movie theaters, grocery stores, or fast food outlets.

Culminating events spotlight the completion of units, projects, and achievements. These tend to be bigger events, and focus on recognizing the service that students have performed, thereby reinforcing the value of youth in society. Examples of these larger events are oral presentations about the project, a book of essays presented to the library, poster displays, a party, a picnic, or an outing. A salient feature of culminating events is their focus on presenting youth as resources and providers of services. Children and adolescents are usually viewed as passive consumers of services. Celebrations validate youth as proactive contributors to the community and as partners in caring for the community.

Celebration goes beyond recognizing the contributions of service learning to student development. It involves recognizing the community for its help in initiating and supporting service learning. Service learning is a community-wide effort that reflects the values, spirit, and concerns of a community. Teachers, principals, counselors, community-based organization staff, parents, and community members are all partners in service learning. Recognizing the contributions of all participants during a celebration validates their participation and contributions. For example, in one school district, the service learning celebration is the community's service celebration. In addition to awards and certificates given to youth, community members and parents are recognized for their volunteer services. The students' response to this kind of celebration is very positive. A community-wide celebration is perceived by them as further validation of the value of service learning and of their value as young citizens.

Celebration creates and nurtures a culture of caring. It teaches youth to care about others in their community and fosters a community that values its youth. It acknowledges students and programs that have made a difference. Sharing successes helps forge links and provides people with an opportunity to show their pride and share their accomplishments.

Preparation, service, reflection and celebration are the elements of service learning. They comprise the process by which a middle school links learning and service. Figure 10 (Kurth , 1995) provides a concise model that shows the application of the four service learning elements.

Figure 10
Field Middle School Service Learning Model

PREPARATION

Identify and Analyze Issues

- Watch the news
- Read the newspaper
- Scan the community
- Hold discussions
- Take field trips
- Talk to experts

Choosing a Project

Types of service

- *Direct service:*
  helping people or environments first-hand

- *Indirect service:*
  channeling resources to a problem

- *Civic Action:*
  taking civic action by working to eliminate the causes of a problem and to inform the public about the issues involved

Learning Service Skills

Basic skills
  - Communication
  - Problem solving
  - Listening
  - Asking open-ended questions

Training specific to an issue
  - Guest speakers
  - Sensitivity training
  - Questionnaires/true or false statements
  - KWL
  - Role-playing
  - Content area studies

Planning service activities
  • Planned with the class and the agency where
  the service will occur

SERVICE

Perform the Service Planned

  • Make adjustments to initial plan as new information
  and circumstances arise

REFLECTION

Individual
  • Journals
  • Scrapbooks
  • Face-to-face meetings

Group
  • Discuss and share experiences
  • Presentations
  • Slide show/video

CELEBRATION

Individual
  • Certificates
  • Pins

District-wide
  • Newspaper articles

The service learning continuum

Service learning should infuse service into the curriculum, not be an add-on program. Ideally it should involve comprehensive planning by faculty, students, families, and community members. But those teachers who cannot fulfill the above should not wring their hands and discard service learning as an unattainable goal, because service learning is not an all-or-nothing proposition.

Most middle schools already have a number of service activities. They occur in many places and take many forms. The key is to identify where this service is already in place and link it to learning. From occasional community service to "ideal" service learning, all service learning activities are somewhere on the continuum. By introducing the key elements of service learning – *preparation, service, reflection,* and *celebration* – existing service activities can be expanded into true service learning.

The four-element model of service learning can be used across the continuum of service activities already existing in middle schools. The degree of infusion is higher as teams integrate service and learning, but it is nonetheless possible and even appropriate to adopt much of the service learning model to all service activities. Thus, students whose service originates out of a club can still experience the preparation, reflection, and celebration components of the model. Likewise, students performing service for extra credit can be involved in these strategies by meeting in groups periodically to reflect on their work and to participate in celebration activities. It is even easier for students in a community service class to take part in most phases of the model.

A continuum of middle school service that starts with a club and eventually expands to a school-wide theme is shown in Figure 11 (p. 43). Note the low infusion – high infusion line below the continuum. The more service that is infused into the curriculum, the more likely it is that service learning will take place as opposed to community service. Again, it is important to keep in mind that community service often leads to service learning. Therefore, school staffs should not feel inadequate if they are only doing community service, so long as the eventual goal is service learning. Below we discuss the ways in which the service learning method is applied across the service continuum.

1. **Service by a school club or organization.** Food and toy drives, math-a-thons, read-a-thons, and intergenerational and peer tutoring are regularly conducted by the Honor Society, Student Council, or various school clubs. Sometimes they involve only members of the group conducting the actual project, but these people

often then involve the entire school in the actual collection of food, toys, or money. While these activities are not service learning, they do help to lay the groundwork for it by beginning to establish a culture of service. Often, students and staff come forward to ask for wider participation in these activities, and insist that this participation not be considered an "extra," but something that is part of the regular curriculum.

2. **Service for extra credit.** Some middle schools recognize the value of service by giving students extra credit for participation. In some cases, the school arranges the service, while in others the students find the service opportunity themselves and then report their work to the school. For this, students receive some credit on their records. Typical service activities of this type include helping in local hospitals and libraries; working in the offices of service, charitable, or religious organizations; and helping at senior citizen centers. These activities are essentially individual efforts and are not usually related to the curriculum. Some call this kind of service "volunteerism."

3. **Service for a special event.** Many community organizations look to schools to help celebrate a special event such as a national holiday (Martin Luther King Jr. Day), a social awareness day (Earth Day), or a community activity (Special Olympics) by seeking students who might be able to help with the event in a community setting. Students are recruited to perform specific tasks at a specific time and place. They may or may not receive training prior to participation. These events are usually highly publicized and are generally recognized as being beneficial for the community. They may or may not provide curriculum infusion.

4. **A community service class.** In still other middle schools, there may be a community service class, either required or optional, in which students learn about the history of and the need for community service in their area and then have an opportunity to become involved in a service activity. Many schools conduct surveys of student interests, which can then be linked to a service opportunity. Often these opportunities are already identified by a

community service coordinator, and students can choose one they like. However, in some cases, the students are responsible for finding the service opportunity. Although this kind of service is not linked to the curriculum, it is linked to the community service class and so, to some extent, is infused into the curriculum. Students also have an opportunity through class meetings to reflect and celebrate, thereby experiencing to some extent the elements of the service learning model.

5. **An outgrowth of the existing curriculum.** As middle level interdisciplinary teams become more experienced, they can use at least part of the school year for a service learning project. In some cases, the planned curriculum is simply put aside for a time while the service activity is completed, while in other schools the existing integrated curriculum provides the basis for a service activity. In this form of service learning, the curriculum is the driving force, and a project that complements the unit is identified. Although there may be a need to rearrange the *sequence* of events in some cases, requirements can nonetheless be covered. This approach may be appropriate where a fairly traditional curriculum is still in place.

6. **A coordinating disciplinary theme.** Instead of forcing service learning to conform to an existing curriculum, some middle schools do the opposite. That is, they select a significant service opportunity that is appropriate to student outcomes and use aspects of subject areas that support the activity and lead to the achievement of stated goals. Thus, the foci of the activity and the student outcomes are on the desired results, rather than on the existing curriculum. In this mode, it is important that the student outcomes have equal stature with achievement of the activity, so that when the unit is completed, both the academic *and* service goals will have been reached. This is because, as important as service is, it must be linked to the overarching goals of the school and not be an end in itself.

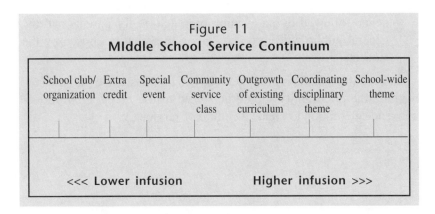

Figure 11
MIddle School Service Continuum

School club/ organization	Extra credit	Special event	Community service class	Outgrowth of existing curriculum	Coordinating disciplinary theme	School-wide theme

<<< Lower infusion   Higher infusion >>>

7. A school-wide theme. Still another stage of service learning, and perhaps the "ultimate" in infusion into the middle school program, is the adoption of a school-wide theme for service. This could be a year-long program or could occupy a limited time, such as the last few weeks of school. What distinguishes it from the two previous approaches is that 1) the *entire school*, rather than just a small team, focuses on the same project, and 2) all subjects infuse it into the curriculum. One middle school decided to stage a circus for the students in a nearby elementary school where there were many handicapped children. The entire school adopted the circus theme and went to work on the project. The theme was the focus of much, but not all, of the learning activities in the various classes. Special subject teachers, especially, appreciated this opportunity to be involved, and thus acrobatics and gymnastics were the focus of physical education classes, while home economics classes made costumes and snacks. Industrial technology classes produced sets, and, of course, the band and chorus provided music for the occasion. Social studies classes studied the history of circuses, while in English class students learned about choreography, staging, and vocal presentation. Science classes learned about the nature and care of circus animals. Students in reading class read about clowns and circus-related topics, and those in math class got involved by calculating logistics. The climax of this year-long event was presenting the circus to the elementary school students, followed by an evening presentation for parents and the general public, with proceeds going to a charity chosen by the students.

So even if a school is not quite ready to infuse service into the curriculum, the opportunity should be seized to use preparation, reflection, and celebration to create a culture of service. Δ

CHAP 4 Organizational Commitment: An Essential

M any avenues can lead to the goal of a middle school culture of service through service learning. It can start in the community or the school, with a club, a special event, a single teacher or team using a service activity as part of one unit. It is not a fixed concept that can only be implemented in one way. Rather, it is an evolving concept that has many possibilities. It is a *process* that can be and is utilized by educators and community professionals whenever they engage youth in service. The distinction of service learning as a process and not a product is important. A middle school doesn't open its doors one Monday morning to suddenly realize that, yes, there is a culture of service with service learning happening throughout the building. Rather, a culture of service is built slowly, over time. The cornerstone for building this culture and practicing service learning is organizational commitment. Other important factors in laying down a foundation are a community assessment, selection of service activities, collaboration with community-based organizations, teacher preparation, and parent involvement. As a middle school's service culture evolves, lots of questions related to advisory boards, communication, funding, and liability are asked by teachers, administrators, school board members, parents, community members, and the students themselves. In this chapter, we explore the cornerstone of the service culture: organizational commitment.

Organizational commitment

Organizational commitment is the core of the service culture. It provides the tangible and spirited guidance, reinforcement, and support needed in the school. It shows that building a service culture within the school is a priority. It will determine the rate at which service is infused into learning through the curriculum. It also defines the degree to which a culture of service becomes part of the school's mission. In this chapter we look at ways to gain the support and commitment of the middle school constituency of teachers, students, parents, and community members. We will discuss two benchmarks that demonstrate a commitment to service learning by a middle school: a rationale statement for developing a culture of service and a service learning activity assessment.

Organizational commitment grows in small ways, eventually permeating the fabric of the school. Reaching this level of permeation, however, is rarely easy. Schools and communities already have full agendas, varied histories of supporting innovative programs, and limited access to service learning information and training. A constant and consistent pattern of decision making needed to build a culture of service through organizational commitment. Open discussion of the benefits and risks of service learning both programmatically and personally will set a tone for the ongoing decision-making process through which organizational commitment will develop. Frequent discussions support the process, helping principals and teachers learn from decisions with poor results and unanticipated consequences and allowing them to celebrate those decisions that strengthen and enhance the school's service culture.

Service learning fits naturally with middle schools. The team concept, mixed groups, flexible block scheduling, and cross-discipline themes provide a supportive foundation for service learning. Furthermore, middle school students developmentally are highly receptive to and motivated by service learning. Service learning and middle schools simply go well together. However, this does not make it easier to gain organizational commitment to service learning. Like any educational innovation, a development process has to take place in building the needed culture.

Organizational commitment may grow from a single event. In many middle schools it starts when an individual becomes excited by the idea of service learning and advocates linking a service activity to a curriculum area. It grows when colleagues, parents, and community supporters show interest in the idea and become involved. They start to discuss expanding service learning to other teams and grade levels. Resources are mobilized. With time, possibly years, resource-brokers and opinion shapers – superintendents, school board members, and union leaders – begin to explore how to change policies, allocate resources, and pursue options. Finally, the community in general notes the changes and embraces the school's culture of service.

Gaining organizational commitment and building a service culture over a period of time requires leadership and champions (Huberman and Miles, 1984; Smith, Redican, and Olsen, 1992).

Even if a school has a rich tradition of community service and volunteerism, the transition to service learning and a strong culture of service is time consuming. Fertman, Buchen, Long, and White (1994) make several recommendations for people who are responsible for building organizational support for service learning and creating a culture of service.

1. **Develop a service learning support system.** Service learning is a public activity. Teachers leave their classrooms and go out into the community, where the potential for problems is increased. People watch what they do. Service learning may entail risks for teachers who are used to working in the privacy of their classrooms. To a somewhat lesser degree, service learning is also risky for the staff of community-based organizations. Their actions too are scrutinized as they move into schools. School personnel often are apprehensive about community people coming in and tend to be cautious. Therefore, a personal service learning support system is needed. The aim of the system is to provide guidance, resources, and support. Middle school teams and principals comprise the natural support system for service learning. It is within the team that the idea of service is germinated and nurtured through cooperation, collegiality, and experimentation .

2. **Be active in the development of service learning.** Service learning changes the roles of both schools and community-based orga-

nizations. It also is part of a changing view of the way schools work and the way children and adolescents should learn. At any one time, service learning may be linked with school reform, apprenticeships, performance-based education, technology education, and substance abuse prevention. Individuals who work to gain support for service learning have a responsibility to stay abreast of changes and developments in the field.

3. **Support discussions.** To expand service activities that are add-on activities into service that is infused into the curriculum, service learning must be discussed at every possible leverage point within the community and school. These leverage points include inservice programs, meetings with administrators, strategic planning sessions, board training, curriculum reviews, and budget meetings. On these occasions a community and school can focus on the role that service learning plays in enhancing the curriculum and promoting student learning.

Discussions about what we want our students to know, how we want them to learn, and how we should assess their knowledge are closely related to how money is spent in communities and schools. The discussions that take place during common planning time should include all aspects of service learning and help make it part of the "core" values of both the school and community. Encouraging these discussions either through formal reflection or informal exchanges helps to support the service culture's development.

Developing a support system, being active in supporting service learning, and encouraging discussions about service learning will help its advocates to face the challenge of building a culture of service. In the short run, these challenges include staff changes, scheduling problems, lack of financial support, and teacher resistance. These issues can derail efforts to build a service culture. In the long run, advocates should recognize that service learning will change the culture of the school. The ability to see change as bringing both risks and opportunities appears critical to gaining organizational support for service learning. Changes should be expected; they should not be ignored or dismissed as incidental to the process. People involved with service learning can and should view themselves as change agents involved in setting direction and policy.

A number of other challenges confront the champions of service learning. The concept of service learning is still young, and many community-based organizations and middle schools are still trying to understand what service learning is. At the same time, they are attempting to differentiate it from and determine its relation to concepts such as performance assessment, community education, apprenticeship, school reform, vocational education, field trips, and class projects. The idea that service learning is a teaching strategy that every teacher might use is just beginning to evolve. It frequently concentrates on so-called "at-risk" students, which is a narrow focus that minimizes the full potential that service learning has as a teaching method.

Service learning competes for teachers' time with every other initiative and the school's daily routine. It has not yet entered the mainstream of school curricula and is even less well known in community-based organizations. Teams do appear to be clarifying the idea of service learning as an instructional methodology, but this has not made it easier for them to apply and practice the information.

School boards and district administrators are often the least knowledgeable about service learning and are less supportive when they do not understand the concept or have misconceptions about it. Cairns and Associates (1995) developed a briefing sheet to use with administrators and board members (see Figure 12). It is a quick snapshot of service learning. The final section in the figure targets board members, but can be modified to target administrators, teachers, or parents as well.

Anderson and Witmer (1994) present aspects of service learning that often concern board members and district administrators. For example, *Should credit be given for volunteerism?* While school boards are seldom opposed to volunteerism, they may believe that volunteerism is an activity that should be its own reward. Students should participate out of a desire to help others, not a desire to benefit themselves by a grade or credit. Responding to this concern, Anderson and Witmer suggest starting to build a school's culture of service by looking for ways to support and expand volunteer activities for students. Schools should keep in mind, however, that service learning is not the same as volunteerism; over and above the service activity it involves both learning and reflecting on the learning.

Figure 12

Service Learning Briefing Sheet
Why Support Service Learning?

What Is Service Learning?

Service learning is a powerful educational methodology that helps students gain and refine academic and social skills and knowledge as they engage in significant service to meet real environmental and community needs.

Service learning encompasses more than community service projects alone. It combines carefully structured educational components with real-world service experience.

What Can Service Learning Do?

A growing body of research shows that well-designed, well-maintained service learning programs can contribute to student learning and growth. Service learning also benefits schools and communities.

- Service learning can build students' sense of self-worth and their ability to make a difference. Students practice critical thinking skills and apply learning in real-world settings. They experience positive relationships working with peers and adults. They also gain exposure to career settings and workplace skills.

- Students are more motivated to learn. Schools gain new community resources. Service learning gives practical form to many widely accepted education reforms.

- Students meet real needs in communities. Youth become lifelong active citizens.

Who Supports Service Learning?

Education-related organizations that have officially endorsed service learning include:

- Association for Supervision and Curriculum Development
- Council of Chief State School Officers
- Education Commission of the States
- National Association of Partners in Education
- National Association of Secondary School Principals
- National Community Education Association
- National Governor's Association
- National Middle School Association

What Can the Board of Education Do to Support Service Learning?

Spell out support for service learning in district mission and goals statements.

Acknowledge and celebrate successful efforts by staff, students, and volunteers.

Link service learning goals with other district goals, such as dropout prevention, use of new technologies, career education, and school/community partnerships.

Provide support for program coordination.

Provide time for planning and organization.

Encourage ongoing evaluation and improvement of programs.

Another concern of boards and administrators is, Will students serve in politically controversial settings? They worry that service activities will cause controversy. Some projects may involve working on a social change agenda, in which an agency tries to correct a problem rather than just providing direct service to those who suffer from it. Some parents may complain if they think their children are serving radical causes. On the other hand, such projects and activities often provide excellent opportunities to help students consider the causes of social problems and to let them know how they can contribute to improving conditions. It may be wise to work in areas that have been identified by the community as important so that community organizations will be more willing to become collaborating partners. It is important to emphasize projects and activities that are hands-on and produce tangible outcomes.

The best way to determine whether service learning is successful is to measure its impact on students' academic achievement, behavior, and overall total development. Each middle school team needs to identify concrete ways of measuring the effects of service learning. Evidence that it does make a difference with students is building (Conrad and Hedin, 1989, Kinsley and McPherson, 1995). Teachers note that students who are involved with service learning are more engaged and on-task in the classroom and during service-related activities. Teachers and principals involved with service learning do not seem to be overly concerned with the need for student success measures. They would like validation that the method has credibility, but they see service learning as one instructional method among many that have desirable results. Service learning helps teachers engage students, exercise creativity, and change teaching routines. However, the ultimate determination of whether a culture of service is developed and sustained is the degree to which it can be shown that it affects student performance in concrete, measurable ways.

Gaining organizational commitment also means capturing the students' interest and enthusiasm for service learning. Students can be super champions of service learning. Again and again, teachers note that students are powerful supporters of service learning. When students talk enthusiastically to people – teachers, community members, and parents – they are heard. As one teacher put it, "What's working is the students' enthusiasm and involvement. Service learning is fun."

Clearly, organizational commitment develops over time. What such commitment involves will vary in accordance with where a school is in the process of developing its service learning initiative. Figure 13 chronicles the service learning developmental process in Mt. Lebanon Junior High School, and shows the organizational commitment required at different points during the process. In this school, service learning was initiated by the assistant principal. Mt. Lebanon had a tradition of community service typical of most middle schools. Food, clothing, and toy drives took place at various times during the year. A number of clubs did short-term service projects. In the classrooms, service activities were limited to letter writing and some cross-age tutoring. Students' volunteer activities were encouraged but no formal support, recognition, or celebration existed.

Figure 13
Service Learning Developmental Process and Organizational Commitment

- Talk with a few teachers about service learning
- Form a team partnership
- Talk with others about developing an activity.
- Invite participation by the principal
- Converse in the faculty room
- Pilot activity by team
- Write letter of support
- Present at a staff meeting
- Survey current school service activities.
- Survey students' volunteer activities
- Solicit superintendent support and recommendation
- Advise the board of education of service learning activities
- Involve additional 7th grade teams
- Present service learning program to the PTA
- Form an advisory board for service learning
- Present to the board and receive endorsement
- Celebrate students' service activities
- Receive a State Department of Education service learning grant
- Initiate service activities linked to curriculum
- Plan service learning community celebration

One essential in determining a school's commitment to service learning is a rationale statement. A rationale statement clarifies a school's reasons for building a service culture through service learning. Figure 14 lists rationales that schools have included in their strategic plans and vision statements for initiating and expanding service learning.

Figure 14

Elements in Rationales Used by Middle Schools for Initiating and Expanding Service Learning

To address students' needs

To link the school and community

To improve academic learning

To increase social responsibility and personal competence

To increase a sense of self efficacy

To promote moral and ego development

To increase decision-making skills

To increase positive attitudes by students toward adults

To increase positive attitudes by community members toward the school

To increase positive community attitudes toward students

To expand career awareness opportunities

To increase civic participation

Often, the rationale is part of the school's strategic plan. When such a statement focuses on learning and community involvement, it provides a strong foundation for service learning. It is an indicator that service learning has achieved a level of organizational recognition and commitment. A strategic plan might include such steps as:

• Establishing an administrative structure designed to implement and manage service learning in the school.

- Promoting service learning in the community.
- Providing a service learning professional development program for faculty and staff.
- Introducing the concept of learning through service on an ongoing basis.
- Recruiting community-based organizations and apprising them of the expectations of the service learning program.

A second benchmark in developing a service culture is an activity assessment that determines the status of the school's service culture. This assessment demonstrates commitment by providing information that can be used to infuse service into the curriculum, modify policies and procedures, and increase support to service learning activities. The assessment process typically includes student and teacher surveys and can be informal. For example, time can be dedicated to brief discussions of current school activities at teacher inservice meetings, or the principal can meet with students informally during lunch. The student council often undertakes the student survey. In schools with newspapers, students may be asked to respond to a brief survey contained in the publication.

Many middle schools prefer fairly formal and structured assessments. These have the advantage of providing more accurate descriptions of the current level of student and teacher activities and list community needs and resources. Furthermore, these assessments provide a non-threatening way to include many different individuals and groups in the process of building the service culture. Finally, they provide baseline information that can be used to design and evaluate the school's service learning activities and measure their progress. Student surveys on current volunteer activities include information on service sites, responsibilities, weekly service hours, and supervisors. An example of a middle school student survey that is based on one developed by the service learning program at Gateway School District, outside of Pittsburgh, Pennsylvania, is presented in Figure 15 with an accompanying letter.

Figure 15
Student Volunteer Activities
Student Letter and Survey

Dear Green Middle School Student,

Reading the local newspapers gives one the impression that the vast majority of young Americans are involved in crime, drugs, dishonesty, violent behavior, or at best are indifferent to fellow Americans.

There is, however, GOOD NEWS in America and that includes western Pennsylvania. There are, in fact, more people giving of their time, energy, and resources to improve the quality of life in this country than ever before. Many of them are contributing as volunteers, which means they are not being paid for their efforts. Eighty million unsung heroes is the figure, says a recent Gallup Survey. That is almost one half of our adult population!

Do you volunteer? Have you done a community service project with the school? Have you done a project with your church or synagogue? The Green Middle School 7th grade team wants to know. We want to acknowledge those of you who have contributed your time and talents to help others in our school and community.

Please fill out the enclosed survey (if it applies) and return it to Ms. Smith in Room 142.

For those of you considering making a commitment to community service, we will be providing you with a variety of opportunities this year to get involved. Check our Green Middle School Community Service Action Board for details. (The Board is located in the hall near room 142.)

7th Grade Service Team

COMMUNITY SERVICE STUDENT SURVEY

Name _____ Grade _____

Home Room #_____

During the last 12 months have you volunteered? Have you done a community service project with the school? Have you done a project with your church or synagogue?

1. Where?

2. What service did you provide?

3. How much time was involved (e.g. hours, days, weeks) ?

4. What do you like about volunteering or participating in the community service project?

The teacher survey presented in Figure 16 focuses on current service activities. Teachers report on their service activities, giving the names of the collaborating agency, the agency contact person, the number of students involved, and the length of involvement. Teachers also note whether or not the service is linked to a curriculum area, a school-wide service activity, a special event, or other school program.

Principals, teachers, students, parents, and community members find the information gained from these surveys both informative and supportive of their efforts to build a service culture. For example, simply tallying and charting the different types of student services provides an indicator of service involvement. Figure 17 lists students' activities from such a middle school survey. Information can also be gathered from agencies where service was performed. At the middle school level, such surveys will include a lot of service through religious organizations and youth groups such as scouts. Data on teachers and classroom service activities direct efforts to link learning and service. Figure 18 is a compilation of teachers and classroom service activities. This information will aid in finding a strategy to involve school teams in service learning.

Figure 16
Teacher Service Learning Activities Questionnaire

Teacher Service Activity Questionnaire

Name _____

Team_____

1. Briefly describe service activities you performed with your students during the past school year (September to June). Please include the names of any organizations and community groups involved with the service activities.

2. Number of students involved:

3. Total time of service activities (e.g. hours, day, week):

4. Was the service (please check and specify):

   Linked to a particular curriculum content area

   School-wide service activity

   Special event/presentation

   Other

5. What are your plans for future service activities?

For example, teachers and teams identified as already involved with service might be a logical choice to target for involvement with service learning. Compiling shown in Figures 17 and 18 at regular intervals (e.g. every 6 months) allows for comparison between periods of activity. Any changes in the type of service activities and the number of involved agencies, teachers, and students can be tracked.

Figure 17
Community Service Activities of Green Middle School Students

1. Literacy volunteer
2. Hospital volunteer
3. Red Cross disaster volunteer
4. Special Olympics volunteer
5. Nursing home friend
6. Recreation instructor
7. School health aide
8. Reader for the blind
9. Humane society volunteer
10. Wheelchair pusher
11. Recycling volunteer
12. Library volunteer
13. Rehabilitation volunteer
14. Day care aide
15. Library aide to shut-in
16. Zoo volunteer
17. Companion
18. Emergency shelter volunteer
19. Server for feeding program
20. Envelope stuffer
21. Storyteller
22. Medical volunteer
23. Clown
24. Signing for the deaf
25. Camp counselor
26. Gift shop volunteer
27. First aid/CPR instructor
28. Home nursing aide
29. Host for foreign visitors
30. Senior citizen helper
31. Museum guide
32. Swimming instructor aide
33. Clothing volunteer
34. ESL teacher aide
35. Blood pressure screener
36. Food kitchen helper
37. Children volunteer
38. Charity fund-raiser

Figure 18
Middle School Faculty Initiated Service,
September to June

- 35 students participated as volunteers in Fall Outing.

- 7th grade team Rooms 242, 244, & 246 worked with the Museum Science Exhibition Program to develop and install the new children's science exhibit. Ten students worked as guides at the exhibit.

- 7th grade team Rooms 250, 252, & 254 worked with the County Feeding Programs to prepare and serve 500 meals at Thanksgiving and Christmas.

- 15 students served as volunteers at the Care Center on 3 occasions and participated in the spring holiday program.

- 8th grade team Rooms 125, 127, &129 worked with the Trail Restoration Project to prepare the 2.5 mile hiking and biking path.

- 40 students from the 6th grade visited the Senior Care Center on May 15 for a day of student-planned activities and visitation.

- A special assembly on "Working with the Homeless" presented by High School students was held for thirty 8th grade students on May 28.

- Also during this time period, school-wide support was given to PALS Writing Project, Valentine Door Decorating at a local nursing home, Special Olympics, and Beta Club Walk-a-Thon for the Healthy Heart Team.

- Students volunteered at the Red Cross collection center for southwest flood victims. A collection was also organized at the middle school. The Red Cross recognized the school with a certificate of achievement.

In conclusion, organizational commitment was defined as the tangible and spirited guidance, reinforcement, assistance, and support provided to a service learning program by an organization. Organizational commitment supports teachers and central office staff to explore the opportunities and face the risks associated with trying something new. Commitment involves helping teachers, administrators, students, parents, boards of education, and community members link service and learning. It calls for the generous and judicious allocation of materials, funding, inservice training, and release time. It leads to the creation of an organizational vision statement and an action plan that links learning and service. Δ

CHAPTER 5

Developing Service Learning Opportunities in School and Community

W hat should be done after you gain organizational commitment to service learning? The next two chapters answer this question. Commitment and interest are essential foundations, but they are not enough to sustain service learning. A community assessment, a process to select service activities, collaborative arrangements with community-based organizations, teacher training, and parent involvement are also needed. In this chapter we look at these elements that support a school's service culture. It may not be necessary to have all of them, but they are nevertheless important and helpful. However, depending on the school, the level of development of a particular item and the mix of items varies. As a middle school's service culture evolves, many teachers, administrators, school board members, parents, community members, and students ask questions about service learning. The following chapter seeks to answer typically asked questions related to advisory boards, communication, funding, and liability, factors to be considered in order for the full potential of service learning to be realized.

Community assessments

Community assessments identify community needs and resources. Since service learning addresses real community needs, completing such an assessment is critical. Many educators elect to identify community needs through community-based organizations such as United Way or local community groups. Others rely on teachers to determine the needs that exist in the community. Informal conversations with community leaders and parents is a third strategy employed by principals. These are all appropriate when trying to initiate and develop service learning. They are minimally threatening, tend to include individuals who are already participating in service activities, build grass roots support for the school's involvement in the community, and strengthen existing relationships with the community.

As the idea of a culture of service builds in a school, one of the ways to strengthen it is to let students complete a community assessment. This is an excellent learning experience, and one that will give students ownership of whatever service activity they eventually complete. Assessing the community is a likely theme for 7th or 8th grade middle school teams to select after the concept of service learning has gained attention and creditability.

When working with middle school students on a community needs assessment, identifying "the community" may present a challenge, because that term can have very different meanings in different settings across the country. While it may be easily recognized in a small town, it may not be in a city or suburban area where students come from a variety of neighborhoods. It is possible that the "need" identified may also specify the "community" where the need will be addressed. For instance, if the need deals with the elderly, then the "community" might be the area encompassed by the school and a nearby nursing home. On the other hand, if the "need" is to tutor local elementary students, then the "community" is obviously more localized.

Community needs can be identified in a variety of ways (Buchen and Fertman, 1994). Students may already be aware of community needs simply through reading local newspapers or watching the news on TV. It is important to focus on local papers and news channels, since these will be more likely to report concerns that the school can realistically address.

Representatives of community agencies may be invited to the school to discuss critical issues that are of concern to them. It is not inappropriate for teachers to "lead" students to a need tentatively identified by the adults involved. They can also look for programs already in place that may need assistance, such as a center for abused women. Furthermore, volunteer centers exist in many communities, often as part of the United Way, that can be invaluable in helping identify needs.

Students may be able to identify community needs through their own observations. Students in one middle school decided to adopt and improve a city park many of them passed every day on their way to school. Where no obvious need is apparent, a neighborhood review can be conducted, in which students comb the neighborhood to identify conditions that seem to call for attention. They will probably find facilities and agencies previously unknown to them that can use their services.

Students can also design and distribute a community survey to identify local needs. This instrument can be administered to students in the school, and through them to parents and community members. Teachers initiate discussions with students about their personal visions for the community and the world. Attention is focused on key issues already on the national agenda, such as homelessness or world hunger.

A second aspect of assessing community needs is identifying available community resources and services. One way to learn more about community resources is for students to talk to people who spend a great deal of time trying to solve community problems. These people should represent several points of view, various levels of responsibility, and varying degrees of involvement in meeting community needs. A list of people for students to talk to would include politicians, business leaders, medical personnel, newspaper reporters, law enforcement officers, educators, community agency workers, and recipients of community services. Community agency workers include staff members of organizations such as boys and girls clubs, drug treatment centers, and homeless programs as well as staff from services mandated by legislation such as child and adolescent services, the criminal justice system, and health services. Another way of learning more about what exists in the community is to secure a list of community agencies and organizations and let groups of students visit them. Keep in mind that students are a resource to address community needs. Pinpoint skills they already have that might be shared, such as reading, math, and computer skills.

Selecting service activities

Selecting specific service activities will be easier after conducting an assessment of community needs. The four steps, also depicted in Figure 19, are:

1. List the existing community needs and resources. Identify gaps in resources and services. Consider the existing community needs that the school or team can effectively meet.

2. Review the topics currently being taught that would benefit from a meaningful service activity.

3. Identify service activities that are already taking place within the school. How might they be expanded into a service learning experience?

4. Consider the students and the ways in which their abilities, interests, and creativity can best be channeled.

Selection of a service activity is not necessarily a formal process and may not even follow the guidelines given above. Some schools make their selection based on interests of teachers and parents who have long-standing ties to community organizations that are working to address a specific community need. In other schools, services activities will find their source in a relationship developed over a number years following a community crisis or activity in which students were mobilized. Special Olympics is an example of a community activity that often leads to ongoing contact between the school, its students, and various community organizations over a period of years.

In identifying service activities, consider two major criteria:

1. **Can the activity involve all of your students?** In Chapter 3 the service element of service learning was discussed. One aspect that was not discussed, however, was the fact that the service activities need to involve all students. Many schools achieve this level of student involvement by mixing the type of service activities (direct, indirect, civic action), staggering the student service activities over a period of a term, and involving multiple service sites.

Figure 19
Selecting Service Activities

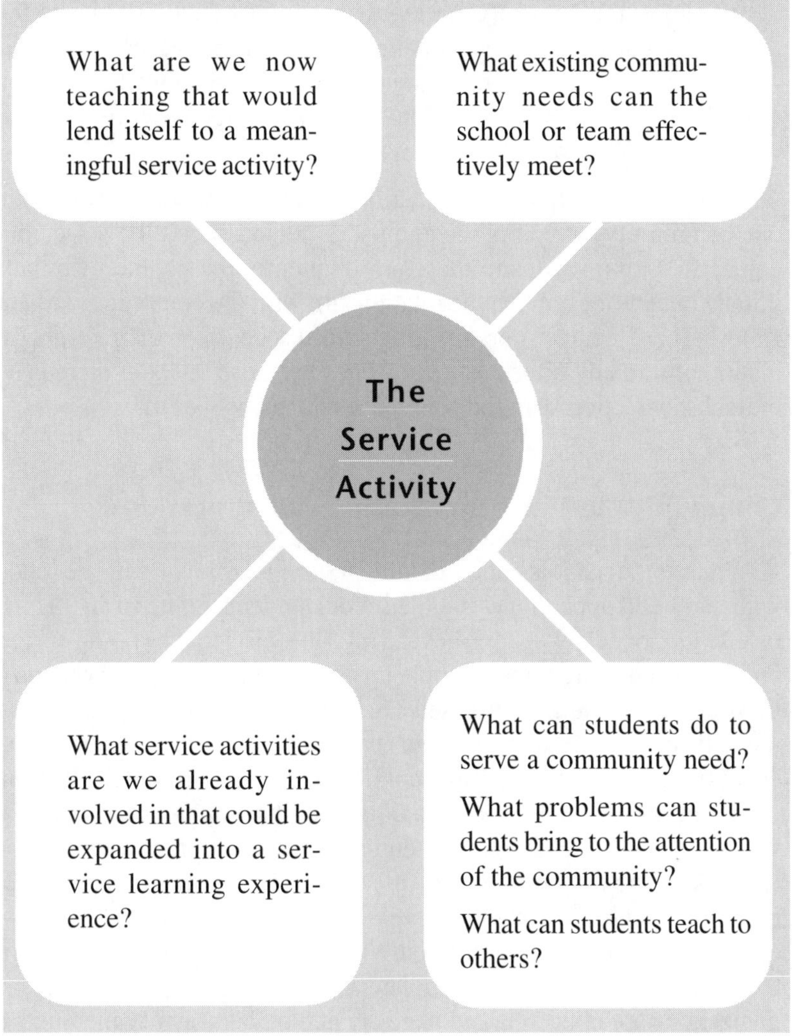

What are we now teaching that would lend itself to a meaningful service activity?

What existing community needs can the school or team effectively meet?

The Service Activity

What service activities are we already involved in that could be expanded into a service learning experience?

What can students do to serve a community need?

What problems can students bring to the attention of the community?

What can students teach to others?

2. Can the activity be infused into the curriculum in at least two subject areas? Linking learning and service is critical. Selecting activities that allow meaningful connections across the curriculum in two or more content areas requires planning by the team. Schools that typically meet with the greatest success strive to find small but varied ways to make connections between each service activity and each content area. This has worked well. A synergy develops that creates additional energy and creativity among teachers, students, and community members.

Once a service activity is identified, one school staff member and one community-based organization staff person should be selected as contacts. Within the team, these are frequently the people who make initial contact or establish the relationship with the community organization. These contact persons articulate the goals of their respective institutions and monitor the progress toward those goals. If there is not mutual satisfaction with the activity, it will probably fail.

Community-based organization collaboration

While some schools build a culture of service by involving one school with another (for example, middle school students going to an elementary school once a week to provide tutoring services) or doing service within one building, most schools involve community-based organizations as well. Community-based organizations and schools are fundamentally different. Although they have common interests in developing capable young people, building communities, supporting families, and improving the quality of community life, their approaches and missions are distinct. Schools and community-based organizations have different hours of operation, professional staff, funding and resources. School existence is mandated by law and supported by taxes. The existence of only a few community-based organizations, such as child protection services, is mandated by law and supported by taxes. Most organizations are nonprofit and were created by community members to address a specific need. These include boys and girls clubs, drug and alcohol programs, counseling centers, baseball leagues, and United Way agencies.

Service learning helps schools connect with these organizations and understand their roles in the community. When planning to work with community-based organizations, the following factors should be kept in mind:

1. **Service learning is new to community-based organizations.** These organizations may have a great deal of experience with community service and volunteerism, but they don't have much experience helping schools build a culture of service. It is important to remember that just as schools haven't had much experience working with community organizations, these organizations haven't had much experience working with schools. Many community-based organizations hesitate to become involved with schools and service learning. There are several reasons for this, the most significant of which is people's natural tendency to resist or react slowly to new ideas. Some organizations are reluctant to work with students they think are interested only in getting out of school. Organization personnel may view youth as troublemakers, and do not believe that they are likely to be very helpful. It is important for the school to be aware of such skepticism. In dealing with these misconceptions, communication becomes crucial. The school must stress to the community agency representatives that service learning goes beyond students' doing a certain number of service hours to meet a course requirement. The misconception that young people are not productive and contributing citizens often takes care of itself once service is underway and it is demonstrated that students, with very few exceptions, can act responsibly.

2. **A school's culture of service has a positive impact on communities**. Besides benefiting students, service learning enriches the community-based organizations participating. Through service learning, community members witness first hand the valuable contributions made by students. The result is that community-based organizations, originally hesitant about having young people in

their buildings, become eager to see them and soon request that more participate.

3. **Collaborations are catalysts for furthering service learning**. The energy and vitality that students offer enhance the relationship between the school and the community. But more than that, the more partnerships that are formed, the more likely it is that service learning will flourish and maintain itself. Greater interdependence through collaboration will also lead to more opportunities for professional development and sharing of ideas.

To achieve the most productive collaborations with community organizations, the following key elements should be considered (Fertman, 1993):

1. **Goals.** Be clear about why you want to work together and identify specific problems, concerns, or issues you want to address. Define the target population that will benefit from the collaborative effort. Likewise, create a timeline for realizing your goals.

2. **Roles.** Define roles for both the school and the agency. Write down individual tasks and responsibilities. Be aware that roles change with time and with each collaborative effort. When problems arise, the issue is not to assign blame, but to decide what roles people and organizations should play in finding solutions.

3. **Balance.** At times, either the agency or the school may contribute most of the resources, but ultimately there should be balanced contributions. Participation need not take the form of direct services – often in-kind contributions, technical expertise, and access to desired resources and information are what is needed. Consider how existing resources are being used to address the problem, and identify where those resources are deficient. Also watch for ways for resources to overlap.

4. **Equality.** Respect each other and work for the best interests of the child, family, community, and school. Each individual should be regarded as a partner with a right to participate in the decision-making process. Recognizing differences and sharing the power

can increase the strength of each participant, as well as the overall effort of the collaboration.

Equality also means giving everyone the opportunity to participate. The involvement of young adolescents is important to their personal and academic development. At the same time there should be adequate preparation and ongoing support for youth and adults to maximize the benefits of their participation.

5. **Trust.** Be candid about both the risks and benefits of working together. A mutual understanding of potential problems and expected benefits may help reduce some of the anxiety that is an inevitable part of a collaboration.

6. **Coordination.** To ensure that plans progress as designed and goals are accomplished, a system must be established to coordinate collaborative efforts. For example, either one person can be assigned to coordinate the work, or a task force that represents all the stakeholders can meet regularly. Signed letters of agreement that specify everyone's duties are also common, while informal gatherings and occasional telephone conversations help to ensure smooth progress. Make sure that everyone involved is fully informed and supports the collaborative effort.

7. **Conflict resolution.** Expect some conflict; it is part of the process. Several types of conflict typically develop. People and organizations that feel threatened by the process engage in turf battles. Conflicts can be as simple as disagreements over when to meet or as complex as issues related to program philosophy. Conflicts arise within an organization. For example, when collaboration results in the possibility of job reassignments or layoffs, or when the staff's workload and schedules are involved, labor union representatives often need to be involved. Conflicts can arise as the partners advocate for new approaches and services to meet the needs of students. These problems should be faced, the concerns of all parties addressed, alternatives sought, and actions taken to resolve the conflict.

8. **Expectations of hard work.** Expect obstacles in achieving goals; these may include resistance to the program, anxiety, and tension. Internal cultures of schools and community agencies sometimes change, resulting in tension. Taking time to prepare individuals to address these tensions and to expect the considerable work that is inevitably involved helps to ensure successful collaboration.

9. **Evaluation.** One of the key benefits of collaboration is the opportunity it provides to gather data about your own performance. Think ahead of time about what feedback and data you want. What would you most like to be able to say about the collaborative effort after one year? In what area would failure most hurt? What pieces of program information do you feel you need to monitor at least monthly, if not weekly? Answering such questions clarifies the collaborator's purpose and identifies concerns up front. The collaboration can then be structured to address these concerns. Periodically revisiting the original goal is also a form of evaluation. Evaluation helps nurture the relationship and also helps collaborators learn from past experience.

10. **The power to change.** Relationships based on a mutual need to address an issue offer unique ways to combine efforts, thus bringing maximum resources to bear. Community agency/school collaborations have the power to change services available for youth. At times the changes are small, such as increased hours of service, while at other times the focus is on adding services such as after school programs, or providing training and incentives to teachers and agency staff. Ultimately, what determines the success of school/community agency collaboration is the degree to which it improves educational and community agency services to youth.

Teacher orientation to service learning

Building a culture of service involves engaging youth in new roles; they become partners in the process, actively participating in setting directions and finding resources. The goal is to help students accept responsibility for the actions they take, to manage their time, develop their organizational abilities, and finally evaluate their progress in all of these areas. Teaching kids to take on these new roles requires a change in the role of the teacher.

Working with students to build a culture of service gives teachers, counselors, and other personnel the opportunity to interact with students in new ways. In lieu of their traditional role, counselors and teachers serve as facilitators of small groups, allowing students to utilize their skills in communication, assertiveness, leadership, group development, and group dynamics.

Counselors and teachers also act as resources, discussing the various service learning opportunities with students. Facilitators may take on the role of a counselor, exploring with students their interests and abilities, and matching these with the various service learning opportunities available. Students may need a teacher's guidance in reflecting upon, evaluating, and making the most of their experiences.

Facilitating service learning with students highlights their varied learning styles. A form of cooperative learning takes place when students work together to serve their communities. To help students work together and profit from cooperative learning, facilitators may be called upon to utilize their skills in conflict resolution. In addition, they must be sensitive to the cultural differences among students. Facilitators can help students feel empowered so that they believe they can contribute in positive ways to their communities.

Counselors and teachers take on a supervisory role in addition to overseeing students involved in a service learning activity. Many work side-by-side with their students in the activities. This is usually a rewarding experience for students, who are able to interact with their teachers in different ways and relate to them as equals. Teachers and counselors benefit by observing students outside of the classroom, where kids feel more freedom to express themselves. Teachers are also able to model pro-social, altruistic behaviors for students in these settings.

Someone from the school may serve as a liaison between the school and other institutions or groups, such as community service agencies, businesses, or churches. In this role, the teacher serves both as a representative of and an advocate for service learning. This might also entail networking with related community-based organizations in order to recruit organizations as service learning sites.

To work with such a wide variety of individuals, people must be skilled in the area of human relations. Mediating between different organizations and participants requires patience, flexibility, honed conflict-resolution skills, and a commitment to the service learning effort. In some middle schools, the role is actually assigned to a particular person under the title "Community Service Coordinator" or "Service Learning Coordinator," who might work at the individual level, the organizational level, or both.

Teachers can serve on the advisory board with representatives from local community and business groups, social service agencies, or citizens at large. Board members' diverse talents contribute to the development of service learning. Their roles will be more fully explained in the following chapter.

Teachers will need to assume new roles within the team as a result of their involvement in service learning. Teams must have a team leader and possibly also a parent liaison, a field trip coordinator, and someone who takes notes at team meetings. An additional role may need to be filled as the team addresses new concerns:

1. Who will be in charge of the service learning activities? The most logical person would be the team leader; but circumstances vary, so the decision has to be local. The person selected must create a timetable for development of activities, ensure that service learning is infused into the curriculum as decided by the team, and coordinate the completion of activities with the partner community-based organizations.

2. What is the team's relationship to the service learning advisory board? If a school has such a board, then a representative from the team should be included on it, both to keep the board informed of

the service learning activities and to take advantage of resources that its members can provide. These resources could include funding, materials, and connections that the advisory board members have in the community. The long-term availability of resources and support is vital and will often rest with the advisory board.

3. How will students get to the activity site? This is a major and often a critical concern. In many school districts the in-kind contribution by the district is in the form of transportation by school bus, which is the safest, least expensive, and most hassle-free method of transporting kids. Private busses are expensive, and many school districts have strict rules about parents' transporting children other than their own. A school may often need parent permission slips even for transportation on school busses.

Finally, as a culture of service develops, additional role changes may take place for teachers. Occasionally teams find themselves with new members who are usually staff members of collaborating community-based organizations. On one hand, this presents an extra challenge to many teams. On the other hand, extra personnel add resources and flexibility. Listed below are a number of roles that team members find themselves performing when the middle school culture of service matures.

- **Change agent.** Service learning is new. Efforts to implement something new are always met with some resistance. Many educators thus serve as point persons in school improvement and restructuring efforts. They act as catalysts by encouraging and empowering students in the classroom and by advocating service learning as a way to make students become more active learners. This may create a need for a person who resolves conflicts, acts as a facilitator, and gives support to staff willing to try service learning.

- **Marketer.** Many people don't understand service learning. Even if they have heard of it, they may entertain misconceptions about what it entails. Teachers should share information with people and organizations about service learning. They will also need to "sell" the school to other community agencies and likewise sell agency needs, convincing the school that they are valid causes to adopt.

- **Lead teacher.** The teachers on one team may be the only group in the school involved in service learning; but as it expands, others will become involved. The teachers already on the service learning team may have the role of guiding others and providing training in service learning. Being a lead teacher involves lots of creativity and risk-taking, but building a culture of service can be exhilarating. Helping colleagues to be creative and adventuresome as they encourage youth to get involved is a critical element of being a lead teacher.

- **Administrator.** Facilitating service learning involves more than interacting with students in the classroom and school. When working in service learning, teachers do many of the same things that administrators do; they serve on the advisory board, meeting with community-based organization representatives and assessing service learning's progress through observations and reports.

- **Budget manager.** Teachers frequently help manage service learning budgets. Some funding typically is required for transportation, supplies, meals, and activities; and teachers are responsible for managing that money. They may also be responsible for writing grants and proposals and managing any grant money that is received. As service learning develops, there will need to be other ways to finance it and ensure that it continues.

- **Community outreach.** Many facilitators involved in service learning are pleased to have the opportunity to get out of the classroom and to learn more about their communities. They are excited to see the community become a classroom.

- **Advisory board chairperson.** A teacher may need to act as the advisory board chairperson, at least in the early stages of development. It is here where the project gets its direction, and community resources can be tapped to support it. We recommend, however, that the chairperson role eventually be assumed by someone else, possibly by someone outside the school.

Building a culture of service in a middle school involves teachers' taking on new challenges. Such challenges can be refreshing, because they provide opportunities to engage in new activities and enter a different environment. However, they can also put staff into unfamiliar roles that call for new skills. Communicating with other teachers who are involved in service learning or working in community service projects can be helpful.

To address all the issues and concerns of teachers involved in service learning, well-designed staff development programs that focus on service learning are important. Figure 20 highlights a program designed by the White Bear Lake School District in Michigan. This district's three level program focuses on the service learning process, building support within the school and community, and linking the curriculum and service.

Figure 20
White Bear Lake School District Staff Development: Service Learning Inservice Programs (Levels I - III)

SERVICE LEARNING - BEGINNING - LEVEL I

Key features:
- 1 $\frac{1}{2}$ day training.
- Suitable for 30 - 40 staff (PK-12).
- Hands-on service learning experience provided.
- Use of Salvation Army Lakewood Adult Day Care Center and overnight retreat facilities of Wilder Forest.
- Level III teachers/administrators and Youth Development Coordinator facilitate the training.
- Funded by District Youth Development/District Staff Development.
- Offered in November or December.

Training Outcomes:
- Participants will be able to define service learning.
- Participants will be able to assess community neighborhood for possible service learning projects.
- Participants will explore an area of service through an actual classroom service learning project in the community.

- Participants will understand the flow of experimental learning, including preparation/training, hands-on experience, and reflection.
- Participants will form a network of teachers within the school district that will share professional growth through the service learning inservice activities and by reporting back on service learning projects.
- All participants will write a curriculum plan (specific lesson plan or unit plan) and carry out a service learning project.
- Participants will attend an after school spring meeting to share results of their service learning projects.
- All participants will receive a final report/curriculum booklet of completed projects.

SERVICE LEARNING - INTERMEDIATE - LEVEL II

Key features:

- 1 $\frac{1}{2}$ day training.
- Suitable for 20 - 25 staff (PK-12).
- Hands-on service learning experience provided.
- Use of overnight retreat facilities of Wilder Forest.
- Level III teachers/administrators and Youth Development Coordinator facilitate the training.
- There will also be use of outside training experts (National Youth Leadership Council).
- Funded by District Youth Development/District Staff Development.
- Offered in October or November.

Training Outcomes:

- Participants will further explore ways of using service learning in new or existing curricula.
- Participants will examine the needs of community agencies.
- Participants will examine ways of orienting students to service experiences.
- Participants will examine ways of using reflection in service experiences.

- Participants will develop strategies for handling the logistical nuts and bolts of service experiences including: transportation, liability, scheduling, equipment, and staffing.
- Participants will continue the development of a support network of educators committed to creating service learning opportunities in the school and community.

SERVICE LEARNING - ADVANCED - LEVEL III

Key features:
- 1 day training.
- Suitable for 15 - 20 staff (PK-12).
- Training of Trainers Experience - Teachers will become trainers for Level I & II inservice programs.
- Use of overnight retreat facilities of Wilder Forest.
- Youth Development Coordinator facilitates training.
- Funded by District Youth Development.
- Offered early in the school year or summer.

Training Outcomes:
- Participants will be given the chance to share service learning classroom (curricular & co-curricular) experiences.
- Participants will create a service learning needs/opportunities list that will be used to support district-level, building-level, and teacher-level initiatives.
- Participants will set service learning curriculum goals for the school year.
- Participants will develop a plan of leadership for the Service Learning In-Service Level I and II training.
- Participants will continue to build a supportive community network of educators committed to creating service learning opportunities in the school and community.
- Participants will have fun!
- Participants will enjoy the beautiful facilities of Wilder Forest.

Redefining the roles of parents and families

The collaboration between schools and community-based organizations that results from service learning helps to build a caring environment that supports children. However, the most important influence in a child's life is still his or her parents. Service learning is an ideal way for parents and families to become involved, because it is collaborative and interactive by nature.

Families can play many roles in developing and supporting a culture of service. The following should be considered when thinking about the role that parents and families play in service learning:

1. **Family members as partners.** Adults in the home can be very good resources in implementing service learning. It is important to recognize, however, that they may be apprehensive about service learning and may express concerns about its value. They may think that it interferes with their child's "real" education. You may hear things like, "Why is my child missing science class to go on some field trip?" or "It's nice that my child is helping others through service, but I want my child to learn what he's supposed to know." These concerns are natural, so it is important for you to listen carefully and communicate openly and honestly with parents about service learning. Stress that students are achieving academic learning outcomes through service learning and make it clear that service learning is not something "special" or "extra," but a part of the student's education.

2. **Families as part of your support system.** You not only want to get approval from the family, but ideally you would like to get them actively involved. The value of parents being involved with their children's education cannot be overstated. One of the goals of service learning is to build a system of service – that gets more people involved in performing service. A successful service learning program, therefore, involves more than just students, a facilitator, and some community-based organization staff. It ought to include family and community members. Let parents know that

they can play an important role in making service learning successful by becoming stakeholders and participants.

Specifically, family members can become involved in service learning activities in the following ways:

a. Parents can act as supervisors at the site where students are working. For instance, at a park refurbishing project students need more direction and supervision than when they remain in the classroom. As adults supervise a project, they also become advocates for service learning.

b. They can transport students in their own cars to service sites when legal considerations can be met.

c. By serving on the advisory board, parents can formally support the service learning activities and perhaps bring a particular expertise to aid the group. A park service activity, for instance, could benefit from having a landscape architect on the board, while a parent whose profession is in social service could help improve a school's relationship with a community organization that serves the elderly or the handicapped.

d. They can help the school acquire appropriate resources. Parents who work in a local paint store, for instance, help in getting supplies to redo a room at a homeless shelter, while parents who work for a paper goods company could help find paper supplies for the shelter. A survey of the families of the team's students would reveal such resources.

The more family members who become involved in supporting service learning, the greater its success will be. Students see their parents or guardians participating, and adults see youngsters learning civic responsibility. As a result, instead of standing isolated from the community, the school's status grows because of its efforts to improve the community. Δ

CHAPTER 6

Reaching the Full Potential of Service Learning

D
eveloping a school's service learning program calls for a consistent pattern of decision making in support of that program. During the process teachers, administrators, school board members, parents, community members, and students ask many questions. Each middle school's experience is different. Therefore, it is difficult to tell with any accuracy when certain questions will be asked or even how they should be answered. Questions arise initially when service learning is just an idea being discussed. Individuals advocating the idea wonder who might be interested and willing to help. There are concerns about time, resources, energy, and other commitments. Questions arise when the service learning activities get publicity, when concerns about students performing service are voiced, when teachers want to apply for grant money to extend service learning in the school, and when students' enthusiasm begins to percolate at home and in the community. At each one of these points, middle school principals and teachers find themselves once again needing to make a decision about the school's commitment to service learning. Is it going to be part of the middle school culture, permeating students' education, or will it be more low key? It is in this decision-making process that issues related to communication, funding, liability, and advisory boards arise.

Advisory boards

Most middle schools have some type of advisory board. These could be mandated by departments of education and have a prescribed membership, purpose, and authority, or be flexible, loosely structured groups of school supporters that may never really meet formally but instead act as support networks for middle schools. The popularity of boards has increased over the last two decades. Their advantage is that they can act as bridges that connect the school, community, and families. The drawback is that they can create extra work.

Advisory boards provide a means for groups outside the school to have limited oversight of school programs and direct access to a portion of the school's program. It is also one way for schools to access resources, support, and technical assistance that would not otherwise be readily available to them. Advisory boards provide a structure for collaboration among the many stakeholders in children's education. Typical advisory boards are composed of the principal, several teachers, parents, and representatives of community-based organizations and businesses. Occasionally, students will serve as board members. In many schools, advisory boards are subcommittees of the parent council or parent teacher organization; in others, they are a separate entity or a subcommittee of a local school board or a community organization's board of directors.

As middle schools build a culture of service through service learning some type of advisory board should be assembled. Service learning involves establishing functional working relationships between schools and communities. An advisory board can act as the catalyst for establishing these relationships. While the benefits of school/community collaboration are many (U.S. Department of Education, 1991), most service learning projects do not start with an established advisory board. Rather, these boards develop along the way. Sometimes they are mandated, but even then they can be slow to form and even slower to become operational.

The questions that need to be asked are: Why form a middle school service learning advisory board? and Is it worth the extra work? The answers to these questions are related to the question raised at the beginning of this chapter: What is the school's commitment to service learning? Middle school service learning supported by an advisory board has a distinct advantage over solo efforts. That advantage is the mutual support that develops between board members and teachers. It is all too easy for one person's commitment and enthusiasm to wane over time, particularly when service learning efforts may not be considered the community's or school's number one priority. The synergy that results when people work together on a team helps sustain their enthusiasm and support of the team's effort, even through difficult times. A service learning advisory board will often be compared to the booster club that supports the local high school marching band. Both support students' learning and performance. In the case of the band, students' musical talents are developed through performing music at community and school events. With service learning, students' academic learning is enhanced through work done with community members.

For the board to be effective, teachers need to view it as a source of help and support rather than a governing body or group of micro-managers. While the board's role is to support and recognize the accomplishment and implementation of service learning, it does not get involved in the day-to-day operation of the school. The board can effectively assist teachers through contacts to: (1) identify meaningful service learning activities, and (2) find resources to complete the service activities.

The responsibility of the advisory board is to support a broad vision of service learning. Once the vision has been developed and clearly articulated throughout the community, the board should work with teaching teams and individual teachers to support the development of service learning goals and timelines. The vision, goals, and timelines link the school and community. Board members and teachers need to be effective spokespersons for service learning so that when questions are raised they can be strong advocates and have ready answers.

An effective service learning advisory board reflects the school's service culture. For example, a middle school with a strong, established culture of service might have a board composed of representatives for the school, local business and industry leaders, key individuals from the various community organizations, and local government officials. Figure 21 shows the composition of an advisory board from such a school. Other individuals who may be of assistance include media personnel, representatives of local colleges, especially if they might later be or are currently involved with service learning, foundation program officers, and representatives from volunteer action centers who can link community-based organizations that want service performed with the educational community. Members of the advisory board would be aware of what is happening in the community, of the skills and services that are needed, and of where those skills are needed.

Figure 21
Middle School Service Learning Advisory Board

MEMBERSHIP: The board consists of:

- 5 student representatives (Beta Club, Student Council, Mediation Center, etc.)
- 1 administrative representative
- 1 teacher from a 7th grade team
- 1 teacher from an 8th grade team
- 1 school board representative
- 1 local government representative
- 1 service club representative (Lions, Rotary, & Kiwanis)
- 1 community service student advisor
- unlimited agency representation
- unlimited community representations (senior citizens, community clubs, religious organizations, etc.)

GOAL: The advisory board meets both formally and informally throughout the school year to coordinate students', community's (borough, citizen, & business) and community-based organizations' efforts to perform the service as an integrated activity.

The board links the middle school with service opportunities that are present in the community. Members work to improve and maintain activities that are realistic and closely related to community needs. The board might include as part of its role the development of broad-based community support, location of funding, and recruiting of students to ensure that they are all involved.

Middle schools just starting to develop a culture of service need a less formal, more flexible support network composed of the people who will be involved in service learning activities. In these schools, the teams need to sit down with the director(s) and staff of the collaborating community-based organization, local governmental officials, parents of children involved with service learning, the students, and the school's principal. These discussions focus on gaining support, figuring out transportation, and making sure that service is linked to a learning outcome.

Over time, boards tend to become more formal. The remainder of this section highlights a number of points to consider as service learning develops and the school's commitment to service learning increases.

Size is an important consideration in establishing an advisory board, and it will vary depending on the scope of the board's responsibility. There is no "best" size. Rather, the optimal size of an advisory board will depend on the size of the middle school and community, the number of service learning activities, and the number of groups to be represented. The goal is to have adequate representatives from participating organizations without making the board unwieldy. Boards usually range in size from about 5 to 20 members. Smaller boards tend to operate more efficiently; however, large boards can function well if officers and key chairs are incorporated into a core committee with subcommittees assuming specific roles.

Selecting an advisory board is an important undertaking and should not be taken lightly. The choices may determine whether or not the board functions effectively. Obviously, board members should be responsible, capable, and committed individuals who are willing to participate. Keep in mind that the board will provide counseling to the team and to community-based organization personnel, and that its members will be in key positions to "sell" service learning to the public. Some important personal qualifications that members should have are:

- a vision for the role service learning can play in the school and community;

- good leadership skills;

- motivation, interest, and willingness to commit to the program;

- strong character and integrity;

- generosity, altruism, and active involvement in community service;

- an ability to express their own values and beliefs, while tolerating those that differ from their own;

- availability in terms of time, health, and location.

Students often serve on service learning advisory boards. They should be viewed as equal members, with the same responsibilities and opportunities for input as other members. It is recommended that boards consist of at least 25% students. This promotes student involvement and validates the idea that students' ideas and work are valued. It is also consistent with the philosophy espoused earlier that students should be involved in their own learning.

As boards become more formal, approval and support may be required from the school board and the administration of the schools involved. Be cognizant of district policies relating to advisory board formation, development of membership criteria, methods of selecting and replacing members, and reporting responsibilities. Even if approval is not required, having the school board recognize the advisory board is a good way to bring service learning to the attention of the school community.

For a board to be effective, its members should be trained so that they understand the scope and possibilities of service learning. Training should focus on the goals of service learning and its place in the school's academic program. You will want to define the roles of members and identify individual tasks and responsibilities. Try to get everyone to participate, but keep in mind that *participating* does not mean board members should provide direct services. Often, what is needed are in-kind contributions, technical expertise, and access to desired resources and information.

Communication and service learning

Since building a culture of service demands a consistent pattern of supportive decisions and actions, it follows that one tenet of such a process must be clear communication about service learning. Communication is necessary for the daily task of building a service culture and establishing an underlying commitment to the value of service for students.

Since service learning involves the collaboration and cooperation of many different groups, communication among the various groups is crucial. For example, in the case of a collaboration between a school and a mental health center, participants may include: center staff, advisory board members, school administrators, school board members, students, teachers, parents, and community officials. Each party will have various reasons for supporting service learning. Some will overlap, while others will not. Each will have concerns unique to its point of view. These views need to be considered, respected, and clearly communicated when planning and building a service culture. For example, Figure 22 identifies the concerns shared by a school and a community-based organization as they embarked on a service learning collaboration. The discussion of these concerns took place early in building the relationship. It set a precedence for communication throughout the project, which continued, spreading beyond the original purpose of the discussions.

Effective communication starts by identifying the people you want to communicate with and the subjects you want to discuss. Students, parents, school and community agency staff, and the benefactors of service activities are groups with whom you want to establish regular, ongoing communication. Communications can be broadly classified into two categories: external and internal. External communication aims to inform the broader community and general school district members of service learning. Internal communication focuses on the process of building a culture of service within the school and initiating and sustaining service learning that focuses on operational details. Both internal and external communications do not have to be fancy or extensive; rather they should be clear, simple, and timely.

Figure 22
Concerns of a School and
Community-based Organization

Community-based organization	School
1. Being able to speak with school personnel when calling the school	1. Developing meaningful service activities
2. Student accountability	2. Verification of service
3. Managing increased demands for service projects	3. Transportation and safety
4. Commitment of students and school working to solve community problems	4. Supervision of students
5. Students being well prepared and trained for service	5. Insurance, liability, and health hazard concerns

Information about the positive things young people are doing is not shared often enough. Service learning can give the community a fresh look at the positive things young people and their schools accomplish. The obvious PR methods like newspaper articles and photos, and time on local news programs are certainly helpful; however, parent newsletters, the student newspaper, formal reports to the school board, and reports to the board of the recipient agency can also be effective. A brief fact sheet like the one shown in Figure 23 can provide a snapshot of a particular service activity or an overview of an entire school service agenda.

Figure 23
Service Learning Fact Sheet

School:
Keystone Oaks Middle School, Keystone Oaks School District

Program:
Service Learning Grounded in Curricula

Location:
1000 Kelton Avenue, Pittsburgh, PA 15216
412-571-6000 extension 6023 Contact: Carol Lucas

Description:
The sixth grade unit on communications that emphasizes the interviewing process combines language arts and history classes. Students conduct interviews with those senior citizens who come to the school on a regular basis for a senior citizen lunch program. They will interview senior citizens in order to create a history of the three communities of Castle Shannon, Dormont, and Green Tree. They will create products that include books, videos, and a still-photo collection that will be displayed in local libraries. They will also host senior citizens in a celebration. As a part of student preparation, the Director of Volunteers for a local senior citizens' residence will speak to the students.

Acknowledgments

—Recipient of Learn and Serve Disseminator Grant—

—Program Recognition in Pittsburgh Post Gazette and Herald Tribune—

—Outstanding District in the Western Pennsylvania
Caring Program for Children- 1993-1995—

—Coordinator named NSEE National Fellow-1993—

Many middle schools in the process of building a service culture produce occasional newsletters. These may include current service activities, recent accomplishments, kudos, personal stories, and details of

upcoming events. An example from a service learning newsletter is shown in Figure 24.

Figure 24
Sample Page of Middle School Newsletter

Corry Area School District

Service Learning Program Newsletter

534 E Pleasant Street, Corry, PA 16407
(814) 665-8297

January, 1995

COMPLETED PROJECTS

Students Taking Action, A. Gernovich and D. Baljo. Junior High students made Christmas cards for the residents at Corry Manor.

Jr. High Advanced Language Class, B. Mancino, and D. Thompson. The Salvation Army's Christmas Dinner was served by students. The classes read a novel and listened to speakers about the homeless before they did this project.

Keyboarding Class, Office Monitors, R. Plemme, and S. Chase. Students entered data into a computer program designed by Dave Edwards. Data will be used to assign Jr. High Students to M&M Day Activities.

UPCOMING/ONGOING PROJECTS

7th Grade Teams and K. Mays. Students will be making picture books out of old cards, calendars, and magazines. The picture books will be given to Rebecca's Home Care Facility.

Jr.& Sr. High Students, S. Mennen, B. Kirik, and D. Baljo. Students are exploring youth center options for the youth in Corry. They are also planning activities for National Service Learning Day and Earth Day.

Word Processing Classes, B. Burr, and D. Anderson. Students from the Word Processing Classes are using their keyboarding skills to enter information into a computer which will make braille for blind students.

**Watch for these dates April 19, 1995 - National Service Learning Day
April 22, 1995 - Earth Day (25th Anniversary)**

Writing newsletters is a learning experience for students because it gives them a forum in which to formally practice their writing. Newsletters also document for participants the things that they have accomplished. A few strategically distributed newsletters may also serve as valuable information to inform community members not involved in service learning. The pieces can display the accomplishments of students and the positive impact that service learning has on both students and the community. In addition, flyers and posters are an effective way to advertise particular activities for the benefit of participants and nonparticipants alike.

Service learning activities can also be publicized through the media. Newspaper, radio, and television should all be used as much as possible. Media coverage conveys a sense of the importance and validity of activities to both the participants themselves and the community that benefits either directly or indirectly from the service. The more coverage service learning receives, the greater the enthusiasm and interest that will be generated in the community. Community cable companies are required to provide "public service" access to broadcasting. As part of their service activities, students can record a video that outlines the issue and describes the services rendered by the students. In addition to its use on the cable channel, the video can serve as a communication tool with civic clubs and other meetings.

Encouraging communication about service learning is the responsibility of everyone involved; it is especially required of the members of the advisory board. Ideally, the advisory board acts as the hub of a service learning activity, where various participants share their perspectives, get a holistic picture of what is taking place, and have a comprehensive interchange of ideas and information. Finally, representatives should share information and opinions from their constituents at regularly scheduled meetings.

Finally, in building a culture of service, the internal communication network among the various collaborators is often overlooked. Of particular concern is communication with the staff of community-based organizations with which the school is collaborating, as these staff members frequently change. New staff will probably have limited knowledge of middle schools and service learning. At the same time, they are critical links to the community and to the success of the project. Meeting periodically with the staff of community-based organizations to monitor the progress of each group of participants, dealing with any real or potential obstacles before they become problems, allowing each group member to give and receive feedback on his/her experience, and to expose participants to perspectives of those functioning in a different capacity will strengthen a collaborative relationship. These meetings are a good time for the organization's staff to update students, staff, and perhaps parents on any new developments. Teachers may want to meet with students within their team in order to check their progress and plan for upcoming aspects of the service activity. The middle school advisory time also provides a good opportunity for such meetings.

Funding service learning

The costs for building a culture of service and instituting service learning are modest, but they do exist, and the issue of funding needs to be faced. Many school districts receive funding from grants given to them by their states. Some funding comes from the federal government which supports service learning through the Corporation for National Service and many federal departments (for example, the U.S. Departments of Agriculture and Transportation). States then make grants to school districts and community-based organizations, some competitively and others based on a population formula. The place to begin the search for funding is the state's department of education office. Check the list of resources with phone numbers and addresses in Chapter 9, beginning on p. 151.

Another source of funds may be local or regional businesses and corporations. This is where the advisory board can be a real asset. Many businesses are happy to support service activities and to get the recognition that comes with that support. It is important, therefore, to market your service learning widely throughout the community – let people know what you are doing, why it is important, and what you need in the way of resources, both financial and human.

Still another way to fund service learning is through the school district or school building budget. When community service is required for high school graduation some resources will need to be directed to this purpose. Since students who have had service learning experiences in the middle school will have greater success with a project in high school, it seems reasonable to ask that at least some of the resources extended to develop service learning programs go to middle schools.

Another proven strategy is to leverage existing federal and state grants that share many similar objectives. Funds from the Improving American School Act, Title One, ESEA, JTPA, Safe and Drug-free School and Communities Act, migrant education, school to work transition, and Perkins Vocational Technical Education have all been used to support service learning as part of the overall categorical mission of the funds.

How do middle schools handle their service learning money? Many employ a service learning coordinator who handles financing as well as finds appropriate service activities for teams and acts as the liaison between the school and community. These people typically work part-time and can either be existing staff members, parents, or community members. One school district advertised this position in the newspaper and was overwhelmed when 35 candidates answered the ad. A coordinator who is not a staff member can serve several schools and usually has more flexibility in contacting the various parties necessary to complete the project.

Other project expenses will likely include materials needed for the activity. Often these can be donated, but some funding may be necessary for items that are needed immediately. As service learning grows, more training opportunities will be available for staff and students, so more money will need to be put aside for this purpose. There is now an annual National Service Learning Conference, and many states have their own conferences. Attending these provides excellent opportunities for those involved to share notes and get new ideas. An effective network is often the most valuable outcome of both the training and conference attendance.

The celebration section of Chapter 3 gives several suggestions for recognizing students and staff involved in service learning. Funds will be needed to carry out recognition activities which may include a meal, certificates, mugs, T-shirts, or hats.

The amount of money needed is really quite modest, and there are many sources of funding for service learning. However, someone at the school needs to actively pursue the funding issue. If the money is to come solely from inside the district, the school's principal will probably have to find the extra money in the budget, which is not an easy task. One consequence of finding money in a school's budget is that someone or something else receives less money. Therefore, the choice is frequently to seek funds from some source outside the school.

Securing funding from outside the school is extra work and involves skills that many principals and teachers have not had the opportunity to develop. As a school begins to talk about developing teacher skills in seeking funding, questions about the level of commitment to building a culture of service arise. To avoid these discussions, many schools try to squeeze a few dollars from the school budget to initiate the project. They look for little pockets of money, or they use PTA bake sale money. Others will look to existing school district external dollars such as Chapter One or school-to-work transition funding and correctly argue that an appropriate use of the funding is to support service learning. However, a strongly recommended approach is for the teachers on the teams to take a serious look at developing and honing their skills in funding acquisition. Figure 25 identifies possible service learning funding sources.

The process of getting money can be enjoyable. You start by finding out about organizations that fund projects in areas that your school already does, or would like to, engage in service activities. The local library is a source of information on foundations and organizations that support educational programs. Environmental organizations often fund environmental projects, and health organizations fund health-oriented projects and activities. The district's central office is also a source of information. Most have a staff person with experience in writing and managing grants. You will probably be able to collaborate with the central office very successfully. Once you have identified an organization, it is essential to know exactly what the funding organization is interested in promoting. Do research on the programs and activities they have funded in the past and the length of time for which they supported those programs. One of the best strategies is to invite a representative of the organization to come to the school to meet with students. Talk with that person about your idea. The immediate goal is to develop a relationship with the organization, let them get to know you, and become acquainted with them.

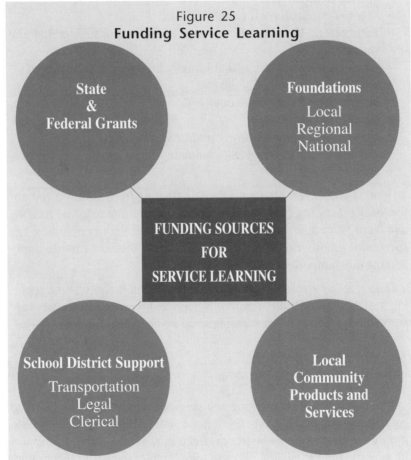

Figure 25
Funding Service Learning

State
&
Federal Grants

Foundations
Local
Regional
National

FUNDING SOURCES
FOR
SERVICE LEARNING

School District Support
Transportation
Legal
Clerical

Local
Community
Products and
Services

The next step is to develop a proposal. Most organizations have guidelines and procedures for applying. Many organizations and most state government and local agencies issue RFPs (requests for proposals). They solicit people to submit proposals for money to fund programs that are of interest to the organization or agency. A proposal typically is a detailed plan of what you want to do and how much it will cost. The following topics are usually addressed in a proposal:

- objectives
- service to be offered
- school coordinator with qualifications
- number and description of students, including their skills and strengths
- times students will be available and where they will be placed
- who will be in charge at the site
- description of site population
- a projected budget
- transportation plan (if any is required)
- provisions for training and evaluating the students and the program

It often takes a few attempts to obtain funding from a source. Ask for feedback on any rejected proposal. Talk to groups that received funding and learn from their experience. Try to network with people who are successful grant writers, since they will know the best time to apply and the most important people to contact.

The goal is for middle school teachers to think broadly about securing the resources to build a culture of service, knowing that teachers are surprisingly successful in securing local and regional funding.

Liability questions

Obviously, students working at a service site may be more likely to get cuts and scrapes or even experience a serious injury than they would if they were sitting in a classroom. Keep in mind that school activities like sports, field trips, and classes (for example, industrial technology and cooking), present the same risks. The benefits to be derived from service learning, however, far outweigh these risks.

There are nonetheless some precautions to take that will minimize student accidents and reduce criticism of school personnel when accidents do occur. Managing the liability for service learning involves a number of steps (see Figure 26, p. 100). The key is to have clearly written procedures and policies that will reduce the risk of injury to your students, and beyond that, taking care not to be found negligent in any way. Adequate supervision is vital. Supervision can be carried out by adults other than school staff members. But adults who are assigned to this task need to be assertive and have clear guidelines of the behavior expected of students. A rule of thumb is that if adults see students doing something they would not want their own children doing, they should correct the behavior or report it to a staff member.

Students need clear direction as well, especially about the use of tools and equipment. The service project may serve as a good opportunity to involve maintenance staff or industrial technology teachers in the proper use of specialized equipment and to review proper job safety procedures. Beyond that, students need to know their immediate supervisor, the physical boundaries for their activity, and the proper clothing or equipment to bring with them to the site. Some schools have found it helpful to assign two or three students to a specific task, much like a classroom cooperative learning experience.

The safest way to transport students to the service site is by school bus. This minimizes the risk of accident and is far more efficient than using private cars. Students will arrive at the same time and can be assigned tasks and given directions all at once. Some districts do, however, permit parents to transport students in personal vehicles, so the owners of the vehicles need to understand that their personal liability coverage needs to be great enough to cover a serious injury if an accident should occur. The school district and its personnel could still be held liable in such a situation, and thus it is wise to review this entire matter with your district solicitor. The transportation policy and procedures on transporting students on field trips of the Boy Scouts of America (1994) provides valuable information to parent drivers.

Figure 26
Managing Liability for Service Learning

1. Have clear written procedures and policies that reduce risk .
2. Ask yourself: Have I taken all reasonable precautions?
   The key is to not be found negligent.
   - master charts that show where students are serving
   - parent permission, release forms
   - clear and adequate supervision and training when needed
   - all drivers covered by the insurance required by district
   - clear rationale for pairing students with the individuals
     they will be helping
   - clear safety/risk management training
3. Make strong links to the academic curriculum (school's mission).
4. Tie service activities to the same policy as work study at
   secondary level.
5. Tie service to the policies of community-based organizations like
   scouts or environmental groups that carry large policies (e.g., class
   becomes an Explorer troop).
6. Check on the coverage of the agencies and groups where you place
   the students. They may be willing to cover the students.
7. Discuss the issues thoroughly with the school's legal advisor.
8. Check with large national insurance companies that specialize in
   volunteer administration and volunteers.
9. Pressure state/federal government to help, since they encourage
   service activities.

You may also want to look into purchasing insurance to cover students while they are at a service site. This would be similar to the coverage provided for athletes when they are engaged in games or practice, or to scout troops when they are camping. It is also possible that the agency being served will provide insurance for volunteers while they are at a site, and this coverage might, therefore, apply to your students. Many school districts permit senior high students to take part in work study programs. The policies established for this program may provide a model for your middle school service program.

The more the service is tied to the curriculum and to the school district's mission statement, the more the project will be seen as an extension of the classroom and, therefore, the less likely it will be that liability questions will arise. In fact, service learning projects are more likely than the traditional "add-on" community service activities to be covered under the district's insurance policy, because these projects are viewed as integral parts of the school curriculum. A wise step is to send a letter to parents or guardians explaining the project and all of the possible concerns, accompanied by a permission slip to be signed and returned. Figure 27, p. 102, provides a sample form. Δ

Figure 27
Sample Permission Form

(Use School District Letterhead)

(SCHOOL)

SERVICE LEARNING WAIVER/PERMISSION FORM

This form must be signed and on file with the building principal before the scheduled date of the service learning activity.

_____

Service Learning Activity

_____

Student's Name

_____

Student's Class   Date

I hereby give my son/daughter approval to fully participate in the service learning activity listed above.

I do hereby waive and agree to hold harmless all school officials for any claim arising out of an injury to my son/daughter except to the extent covered by accident or liability insurance.

A parents or guardian's signature is required to validate this document. Please sign below.   _____

                                                    signature

Service Learning is being offered as an alternative learning experience by the _____ School District under the provisions of 22PA. code Chapter 5 sections 5.214b and 5.222d.

CHAPTER 7

Sustaining a Service Culture

W hen any new program is introduced in a school, people will have questions. They want to know what it is, what it does, how much it will cost, how much work it is, how the work is done, whether it will be required, whether it will be replacing anything, and, of course, whether it works. The answers to this string of questions help people decide if the time and effort needed to implement the program are worthwhile. For people who already advocate and champion the idea, the answers to these questions provide support and feedback. The information tells them how they are doing, what is working, and what isn't.

Lots of answers to the questions asked are self-evident and intuitive. *Yes*, students are learning; *yes*, service learning is working; *yes*, teachers are including it in their curricula; *yes*, students, parents, teachers and community members are excited about the program. However, at a certain point in the evolution of the service culture and service learning, the cheerleading, flag waving, and testimonials based on the personal experiences of students, teachers, and community members lose their power. Principals, teachers, community members, and students need and want a greater amount of more and varied information and feedback. In this chapter we explore ways to fulfill the need for assessment information and feedback through evaluation.

The idea of building a culture of service captures the imagination of many people: teachers, students, parents, principals, central office administrative staff, and community members. They like the idea. However, the degree of interest, commitment, and involvement will vary. Therefore, their questions and need for information will also vary.

Those already committed to service learning will need information on how it is functioning. With that information, they can determine what should happen next to strengthen the school's service culture and commitment. They need information to help call attention to the successes of service learning. Furthermore, they need to think about what has been learned through their experiences so that they can refine their work.

Colleagues and community supporters need information that will help them decide how to collaborate in establishing and promoting a culture of service. They need answers to their questions so that they can join the planning process and help mobilize resources. To overcome their initial anxieties and fears, the information needs to be reasonable and non-threatening.

Resource brokers and opinion shapers such as school board members, elected government officials, and community leaders need information that will persuade them to consider changes in policy, resource allocations, or program activity.

The community at large desires information on what is actually being accomplished. They want to know about the tangible outcomes; for example, did the children learn more, did they conduct themselves properly? Furthermore, the general public wants to know the impact of service learning on the community; for example, is there an increased sense of pride and civic responsibility among community members in neighborhoods where service learning activities take place?

To answer all of these questions much data are needed, including a description of the program's goals and desired outcomes, general information on the students and service activities, the ways in which everyone is working on building a school culture of service, and the impact of service learning. In addition to answering people's questions, this information serves as the basis for ongoing planning and development of activities that lead to improved practice.

Goals and desired outcomes

The first step in answering questions about service learning in your school is to have a clear and concise specification of the goals and desired outcomes of a service learning program. You need a clear statement of:

- what you want to accomplish
- for whom
- with what effect

It is important to be honest and realistic in listing what you hope to accomplish. Figure 28 is a worksheet that is helpful in identifying goals and desired outcomes. While it is easy to write down many different goals on the worksheet, remember you will be evaluated on those goals, so they should be realistic. In addition, it is easy to revise your original goals should response to your program be less than you had hoped. Since the evaluation process is designed to provide feedback on how to improve service learning and to help you understand why your original goals were not accomplished, it is best to be as specific as possible in the initial step of evaluation. When you write the synthesis for the benefit of the community, it pays to be honest and realistic. Think through what the activity involves, and ask yourself, What would we like to have happen as a result of this? What is reasonable to expect given the intensity, frequency, power, and length of the service learning activity? How do we expect the students to change?

Establish an accounting system to maintain basic records on the number of students involved, classroom periods used for preparation, reflection and celebration activities, and the breakdown of service activities by tasks. In its simplest form, such a system records student hours; but more sophisticated systems can include service activity tasks, site, beneficiaries, and learning objectives. A record-keeping system allows for scrutiny of activities and identification of strengths and weaknesses. A group of students could design this record-keeping system. This would help establish ownership for the activities and allow students to practice organization and computer skills. The following are sources of desired information:

- parent permission forms with room for feedback about the service activities
- a master calendar showing current and future service activities
- a site record of student activity
- a record of total hours of service provided
- written observations by student participants
- feedback forms detailing experiences from service recipients
- feedback forms from teachers and site directors related to the service activities

Many schools design simple forms that a teacher or team completes at the end of a project and keeps as part of the team's records. In schools with a service learning coordinator, the forms might be collected and summarized. Figure 29 shows a sample report form.

Figure 28
Identifying Service Learning Goals and Desired Outcomes

TEAM _____

DATE _____

Part A – Service learning goals
What do we want students to learn? Specify the desired learning outcome.

Part B — Service learning activity
What is the service learning activity? Include the community problem to be addressed and the collaborating community-based organization(s).

Part C — Product or synthesis
What kind of product or synthesis will enable students to integrate significant learning?

Part D — Community benefits
What are the tangible and measurable community benefits?

Figure 29
Service Learning Program Activity
and Project Report

SERVICE LEARNING PROGRAM ACTIVITY AND PROJECT REPORT

Name _____

Team _____

Activity / Project _____

Number of Students Participating _____
1. What is the number of hours each student participated in this project?

2. How many of these hours were actual service hours?

3. How many of these hours were learning hours? (Note: Numbers 2 and 3 should equal Number 1.)

4. Number of beneficiaries of this project_____. Who were they? (In other words, how many people did you serve and what group(s) did they belong to?)

5. Did any parents assist you in this project? If so, how did they help, and how many parents participated?

Summarizing the basic information so it is manageable and usable is a concern of many principals and teachers. It needs to be in a form so that the various requests for information can be accommodated. Colleagues and community supporters want information that will help them decide whether to collaborate and promote a culture of service. School board members, elected government officials, and community leaders need information to consider changes in policy, allocation of resources, and program activity options. The community at large wants information on what has actually been accomplished. Figure 30 shows a Service Star Report (Fertman, 1993) that was developed to help schools summarize basic service learning information. It is used to help focus discussions about service learning on areas that are critical to all who advocate and champion service learning activities.

Figure 30
Service Star Report

	___ Elementary ___ Urban
	___ Middle ___ Rural
Tel: ( )	___ High ___ Suburban
Fax: ( )	___ College
Contact:	___ Other

Number of Student Participants	Service Hours	Learning Hours	Total Service Learning Hours

Advisory Board
Number of meetings:
Number of members:
Number of students:
By-Laws? ___ yes ___no
Committee Structure?
      ___yes ___ no

Curriculum Infusion
Teachers/Staff Involved:

Content Areas:

Training
Coordinator Hours:
Number of Staff Trained:
Staff Hours of Training:
Trainer(s):

Student Success Measures

Agencies   #:
List:

Parental Involvement
Parents Involved:

Parents on Advisory Board:

Beneficiaries   #:
List:

Products	#	Topics
Videos		
Brochures		
Other		

Service Activities

Service Star Report

The *Service Star Report* is a concise reporting tool that can be used to describe a service learning program in very concrete terms. It captures all the critical elements of service learning. Completing the report allows you to see where a program is now and where it is going.

The following terms used on the *Service Star Report* may require some clarification:

Service hours: Time spent by participants actually doing service activities.

Learning hours: Time actually spent by participants in preparation, reflection, and celebration activities.

Service learning hours: Sum of all service and learning hours (total hours, not hours per participant).

Advisory board: The group of people organized specifically to help coordinate and advocate for service learning.

Training: Training or instruction in service learning provided. This covers a wide range of activities, including workshops, meetings, and conferences.

Agencies: Agencies with which you are involved as part of your service learning program. These are ongoing, formal linkages. Provide both the number of agencies you're involved with and a list of these agencies that are most significant to your program.

Beneficiaries: Provide both the number of beneficiaries and a list of the primary ones. Be realistic. Focus on those people who have directly benefited from the service.

Curriculum infusion: How service learning has become an integral part of the curriculum. Tell which content areas in your school have included service learning in their curricula. List the subjects that have integrated it into their lesson plans. How many teachers or other staff members are involved?

Student Success Measures: How you evaluate the effect that service learning is having on students. What are you looking for to show that service learning is worthwhile and effective? Keep in mind that self-esteem and positive attitudes are important as measurements of success, but much better are grade improvements, reduced absenteeism, increased interest in school, and improved behavior.

Parental and family involvement: Families can be involved with service learning in several ways. One parent may attend a celebration event once, and another may actively assist with service learning activities on a regular basis. Include them both.

Products: As your program develops, it is important that you talk about it and display successes to other people. Have you put together any informational materials on service learning at your school or community-based organization, such as a video, brochure, poster, or report? If so, list them.

Service activities: Concise list of all service activities, with an emphasis on activities that are linked to the curriculum.

Working to build a service culture

Once the basic information is acquired, the next step is to establish a dialogue about how everyone is working to build a school culture of service. For example, feedback is needed from the key staff involved. Typically, staff members report their lives become busier, but that they have more personal satisfaction and excitement about their jobs. While this is positive, it is important to be careful that staff don't get so busy that the extra work involved in service learning becomes a burden. Principals, administrators, and community-based organization directors who support the link to the bigger organization are another important source of feedback. Competition for their time and energy is often keen, and service learning can mean more work for them. To maintain an ongoing dialogue about service learning, be respectful of people's time. A one or two question survey is a useful tool to collect information. Holding a brief focus group once or twice a year is also effective. Students should be included, since they can provide unique answers and views that contribute to the success of service learning.

Evaluation questions can be used in a survey or focus group. The goal is to obtain a quick snapshot of what is happening, summarize the results, and report back to people promptly. For example, you can write a mini-report which can be distributed to teachers, administrators, and community-based organization staff. Figure 31 is an example of such a report. If students were surveyed, the results could also appear in the school newspaper.

Sample evaluation questions for staff:

1. What's working with service learning?
2. What are three DO'S for a successful service learning activity?
3. What are three DON'TS for a service learning activity?
4. What effect is service learning having on your students?
   Concentrate on:
      a. involvement/engagement in learning
      b. application of skills and knowledge
      c. appreciation for civic responsibility
5. What change, if any, have you seen in the attitude of community members about young people as a result of service learning?
6. What impact has service learning had on the philosophy and/or program of the school?
7. What impact has this experience had on you?

Sample evaluation questions for students:

1. What do you like about service learning?
2. What skills have you used or learned during the service activities?
3. How much input have you had in creating and carrying out the service learning project?
4. What effect, if any, has work on the service activities had on your work in other subjects?
5. What would you suggest be done to improve the service learning experience for other students?

Figure 31
Service Learning School Mini-Report

Green Middle School Service Learning Update

A group of 14 teachers from two teams met recently to discuss how service learning is progressing at Green Middle School. We asked ourselves the following two questions:

1) What's working?

2) What problems are we facing?

Here's what's working:

Strong advisory board. The advisory board formed last year has expanded to include five more members, including two parents and Joseph Krebs, President of the Green Area Chamber of Commerce. Board member May Smith met with the Animal Rescue League to discuss a new 8th-grade service activity.

Parental involvement. Parents of Green students are involved in service learning. Several are serving on the advisory board. But more than that, they are gradually becoming more invested in service learning. Five parents have been involved at celebration activities and two have been lending their time and professional experience to various service activities.

Acceptance by teachers who are not yet participants. Service learning at Green appears to be gaining greater acceptance by teachers who have not previously been involved with it. In the past, service learning was met with opposition by a few teachers, who viewed it as simply an add-on that would give them more work without any real rewards. Now, these teachers are realizing that service learning is not just an add-on; it can play an invaluable role in everyday learning.

The problems we face:

Transportation. Getting students to service sites continues to be a problem. There is little money in the budget for transportation. Parents have helped to alleviate the strain somewhat, but the liability issues make relying on parents difficult.

Time constraints. Teachers need more time to implement service learning effectively. Other responsibilities and commitments make it difficult. Our push toward infusing service in the curriculum should ease these burdens, but for now teachers and students need more released time to make service learning work.

Marketing. Although the advisory board has begun to expand into advocacy, the positive benefits that service learning provide, both to students and the community, are not being picked up on by the community. The local media focuses on negatives in the school and school district and does not take the time to see what a positive story service learning could be.

Student outcomes

Part of maintaining an ongoing dialogue about service learning in a school and community is sharing information about student outcomes. People want to know if service learning is worth the time and effort it requires. Does it make a difference in student learning? For instance, when students involved in service learning are compared with students taught with non-service learning methods, do the former get better grades, have fewer behavior problems, graduate from high school more regularly, and pursue more post-secondary educational options? These are questions the school and community want to have answered.

The information needed to answer these questions can be gleaned from surveys, writing assignments, student records, and teacher observations. As part of their regular reflection period, students can discuss the impact that service learning has had on their lives. An excellent way for students to evaluate their own growth is to keep a service learning portfolio. It serves as a historical record of their accomplishments and provides a record of their learning as well. Individual conferences with students and parents are also a way to evaluate the program. The reflection process described in Chapter 3 provides a further opportunity to obtain student feedback on the overall effectiveness of the service learning experience.

When evaluating student outcomes, it is important to remember that academic learning and personal development represent the core of service learning's student outcomes. For many, service learning offers transforming experiences that empower students, bring life back in their school days, and instill in them a desire to learn and succeed. This is because it is a "real" experience and puts students in the role of a worker, with the teacher as coach. In addition, it is important to assess whether involvement in a service experience affects a student's commitment to the community, his or her self-esteem, and most importantly, his or her sense of self-efficacy. For example, observation of existing service activities verifies that service learning can have an especially positive impact on the self-esteem and self-efficacy of special education students and students with a history of discipline problems.

Realistic expectations are critical to the evaluation process, particularly in the early developmental and implementation phases of a program. Service learning is not the answer to all learning and school problems; it is one strategy among many that schools and communities use. Aware of the need to be realistic, many schools initially emphasize outcomes related to absenteeism and disruptive behavior. Since assessments show that students' being part of service activities correlates with a decrease in absenteeism and behavior problems, this often leads to more opportunity to learn and may ultimately be linked to better academic performance.

This focus leads schools to construct and utilize self and teacher attitude and behavior rating scales. Figure 32 shows a self-rating attitude scale used before and after a unit that was taught using service learning. Figure 33 shows a rating scale that teachers can use to evaluate students' behavior while performing service. This form can also be used as a self-rating scale by students. It can be repeated at intervals during a single service activity, or over the course of a number of service activities. Such scales can also incorporate items from the U.S. Department of Labor's listing of "workplace know-how" (S.C.A.N.S., 1993) and new educational standards under development (Kane & Khattri, 1995).

Figure 32
Self-Rating Attitude Scale

Community Service Survey

Circle the phrase or word that best describes you.

1. I like to work with others.	lots of times	sometimes	seldom/never
2. I like to help people.	lots of times	sometimes	seldom/never
3. I like to help people with problems.	lots of times	sometimes	seldom/never
4. I think my help is worthwhile.	lots of times	sometimes	seldom/never
5. I feel comfortable talking with adults.	lots of times	sometimes	seldom/never
6. I feel comfortable working with adults.	lots of times	sometimes	seldom/never
7. The things we study will be useful to me someday.	lots of times	sometimes	seldom/never
8. I have some ideas about what I want to do when I grow up.	lots of times	sometimes	seldom/never
9. I can help my school.	lots of times	sometimes	seldom/never
10. By helping in my community, I can make a difference.	lots of times	sometimes	seldom/never
11. I like to do things that help the natural world survive.	lots of times	sometimes	seldom/never
12. I like to try new things.	lots of times	sometimes	seldom/never
13. I am good at solving problems.	lots of times	sometimes	seldom/never

Name_____ Date_____

Source: Woo, 1994

Figure 33
Rating Scale to Evaluate Students

STUDENT VOLUNTEER EVALUATION FORM

NAME_____

Please rate the above student's performance in the following areas. Ranking the individual questions on a scale of 1 to 5, using the guidelines listed below.

1	2	3	4	5
unsatisfactory	poor	fair	good	excellent

These ratings will be treated as valid judgments and will be calculated in the student's grade for the service learning project. Please be as fair, honest, and objective as possible, as you would be with an employee. The students need to see that performance is tied to reward, and that true self-esteem cannot be given or taken – only earned!

WORK HABITS

1. Followed rules and regulations._____
2. Performed tasks efficiently, did not waste time._____
3. Demonstrated accurate record handling._____
4. Was punctual, on time for duties._____

ATTITUDE

5. Asked relevant questions, showed interest._____
6. Was polite to staff and public._____
7. Showed an open mind to learning and criticism._____
8. Was helpful to staff and public._____
9. Exhibited a willingness to listen to others._____
10. Demonstrated cooperation with staff, public, team._____
11. Took role seriously, made a real effort. _____

PERSONAL SKILLS AND TRAITS

12. Dressed appropriately for the environment._____
13. Was clean and well-groomed, good hygiene habits._____

14. Displayed age-appropriate maturity, responsibility._____
15. Communicated clearly and correctly to all contacts._____

OVERALL OPINION

Because of the subjective nature of these evaluations, an area where an overall judgment of the student must be recorded is included. That may be done individually by a department supervisor, or as a joint decision by all involved staff members. Please feel free to work in any way most comfortable to the co-ops in your department.

(This overall rating should be on a scale of 1 to 20.)

16. Overall opinion _____

Total rating (sum of 1-16) _____

Student Name   _____

Evaluation Date _____ Team_____

Staff Names _____

Please feel free to make appropriate comments concerning the student, the program, etc. All suggestions are welcome.

_____

_____

As part of trying to evaluate student outcomes, use of alternative assessment methods was mentioned above. In the very areas where real progress is most difficult to measure, such as language arts and social studies, service gives students experiences that will demonstrate whether they have acquired the knowledge and skills identified as important. It provides validity to assessment, while helping students understand that what they have learned is useful in the real world. Service learning is particularly well designed for the use of performance assessments. Furthermore, it provides a way to evaluate skills such as knowledge integration across disciplines, contribution to the work of a group, and development of a plan of action when confronted with a new situation.

Service activities enable a number of students to work together on a complex problem that requires planning, research, internal discussion, and group presentation. Opportunities for public presentations to various groups concerning the activities, accomplishments, and learnings are often available. In many schools, creating an orientation video helps to acquaint students, staff, the school board, and the public to service. Developing the video also serves as an occasion for reflection.

Demonstrations based on service activities provide students with opportunities to show their mastery of subject-area content and procedures. Students in a science class might, for example, demonstrate their experience in growing plants for a nature center or park. Students in a health course could demonstrate mastery of the techniques necessary for caring for patients in various stages of recovery at the hospital where they perform their service.

In order to fully implement performance assessment, administrators and teachers must have a clear picture of the skills they want students to master and a coherent plan for how students are going to master those skills. They need to consider the way students learn and what instructional strategies are most likely to be effective. Finally, they need to be flexible in using assessment information for diagnostic purposes to help individual student achievement. Because service is real and authentic, it presents many opportunities for students to demonstrate proficiency in lifelike, work-related settings.

Impact of service learning

Substantive questions often arise about the impact that service learning has on community members. To answer these questions, it is best to solicit information from various sources about the impact of service learning. Visits to the service sites, regular telephone discussions, and written evaluations are sources of relevant information. Service beneficiaries are not the only source of such information. Frequently, individuals not directly involved with the activities receive some benefit and willingly share their reactions. Site supervisors, community and agency representatives, other students and volunteers, and parents may be beneficiaries. Another measure of impact is the extent of involvement in service learning. Recording the number of teachers and community agency staff involved provides one indicator of its acceptance and dissemination within organizations. The total number of organizations involved is another indication of community impact.

Ongoing planning and development activity

The ultimate purpose of the information gathered in assessments is to improve service learning, whose goal in turn is to further young adolescents' learning and development. Typically, teachers use the information to adjust service activities to meet curriculum objectives, tailor training to student needs, and strengthen reflection. The information is used in team meetings to ensure that academic goals are being met and students are engaged. Likewise, sharing information with students, parents, community members, and administrators while soliciting their input helps to strengthen the service culture of a school. It assures that needs identified by the community are being addressed through collaboration between the school and community.

Evaluation information is a critical element in the planning process; it provides a basis for continuous improvement and helps to ensure quality education. It supports curriculum improvement, promotes the exploration of new possibilities, and encourages experimentation. Evaluation is essential in building a service culture that links learning and service. Δ

Case Studies of Service Learning in Action

S ervice learning is taking place in many middle schools throughout the country. It can be found in small and large schools, in rural, suburban, and urban communities, under the leadership of individual teachers, teaching teams, and school/agency partnerships. In this chapter, five case studies illustrate the fact that there is no one right way to build a culture of service and implement service learning. The following guide will assist you in identifying the common threads that bind these middle schools' programs together.

Guide to reading the case studies

As you read the case studies think about the information that will be useful as you implement service learning in your school. In each case study look for the following:

- Descriptive information. The name of the program(s), the contact person and his/her address and phone number, the number of students involved, and the number of individuals in the community who are connected to the program (both as helpers and recipients of service).

- Description of the service experience. What are the service activities all about? What do students do? What have the results been? What value does this type of experience have for students and community members?

- How the service is infused into the curriculum. Identify the types of service and expected learning outcomes. What subject or specific units in this subject are connected to the service.

- How did the school and/or district demonstrate organizational commitment to service learning?

- What obstacles had to be overcome as service learning was developed and implemented (e.g., transportation funding, insurance, community attitudes, etc.)? How did the teachers deal with these obstacles?

- What were past traditions of service upon which service learning was built? Has service learning enhanced the culture of service in the school and community?

- How are families informed of and involved with service learning?

- What is the cost of implementing service learning? How were these costs funded?

- How has service learning changed the way schools and community organizations interact (e.g., have agencies made modifications so that students can become involved)?

- Is there an advisory board in the school or district that oversees service learning? If so, what is its role? Who are the members? How are they selected?

- Who coordinates the program; a teacher or community member? Is the position paid or unpaid?

- How has service learning been evaluated?

Martin Luther King, Jr. Academic Middle School. Report by April Holland, seventh grade teacher.

It is Friday at this multi-ethnic inner city school in San Francisco created by the Department of Integration. Today everyone is rushing around preparing for our first full-fledged Service Day. I meet Susie Floore in a corner of our school resource room, which serves as an office for our three partners from Partners in School Innovation. Susie teaches science to four seventh grade classes. I teach the same children English.

Susie asks Rand Quinn, one of the partners, "Did you arrange for bus tickets?"

"Oh my gosh!" I interject, "I didn't even think to ask."

Josette Cordova, another partner, hands us both tickets. We breathe a sigh of relief and prepare to go to our classrooms. We bump into Ann Clemenza coming in as we leave. She's the science-math teacher for the other two strands of seventh graders.

"Do you know how many buses it's going to take to get my kids to Fort Funston? If I don't get a grant for school buses for these once-a-month trips, I'm going to have to find a new site. We're going to spend all day today on the bus," she muses.

"You know, we should find out about the Linking San Francisco grant any day now," our third partner, Britt Anderson says. He always exudes optimism (in this case well placed, as we were one of twelve Linking San Francisco schools to receive a grant for over $2,000 for busses and supplies).

Thank goodness for the partners! These three young college graduates came to our school via Partners in School Innovation, a nonprofit organization designed to support new and creative approaches to education. They work four days a week at our school on the seventh grade service learning project and the seventh/eighth grade peer resources elective. On Mondays, their only day off-campus, they meet with partners from other schools and receive training to make them more effective in their support roles. They receive a stipend, which covers basic living expenses.

The first morning bell rings, and students flood into the building. You can feel the excitement as the seventh graders hurry into their special service homerooms. All seventh graders will be leaving the campus today, traveling in six different directions to perform service of six different kinds.

My service homeroom will take a very short bus ride to the Whitney Young Child Development Center. There, the students will be divided into the five preschool classes and serve as young aides to the nursery school teachers. I feel very comfortable with this site, since I worked with them two years ago when we started service visitations.

Ms. Floore probably feels confident as well, since her homeroom's destination is also a repeat – Candlestick Point Recreation Center. This time, the students will complete architectural plans and actually break ground and begin building the foundation of an amphitheater there.

Francine Donner, who teaches an English/social studies core to two strands of seventh graders, will walk her service group across the street to E. R. Taylor Elementary School. Although they worked with us two years ago, Francine was not teaching seventh grade at that time, so this will be new to her. Her students will be aides in fifteen or so elementary school classrooms.

In Viki Gonzalez's room, usually blustering with social studies or Spanish classes, students will be learning about neighborhood cleanup procedures from the San Francisco Clean City Coalition in preparation for their hands-on local beautification efforts. This is a brand new service site for our school.

Across the hall in Arva Robinson's class, instead of the usual math lessons, the youngsters will be involved at one of two sites where they will feed the hungry. Two years ago, Arva directed students in the hand sewing of a quilt which was donated to a homeless shelter.

Ann Clemenza has many big plans for work at Fort Funston, the farthest site from our school, at the opposite end of San Francisco. Luckily, she has Max Foreman along to help chaperone the restless bus riders. Max teaches a special day class of severely learning-disabled students, but since we have incorporated all of his students into the service homerooms, he is available to help out. Similarly, Mary Janigian, the special education teacher who follows the other learning-disabled seventh graders, is free to go along with Arva Robinson. The rest of us also have adult support from the partners and a United Way support person (formerly paraprofessional). Believe me, with thirty or so students per service site, the extra supervision is very helpful. Two years ago, when just four of six seventh grade teachers were involved, we didn't have this luxury.

Two years ago, we were just starting "communities." This is where distinct strands of students travel together to each of their four academic classes. The math, social studies, science, and English teachers of these students have a common preparation period. Before this, students traveled randomly from class to class, and teachers only had common time before or after school. Four of us decided to meet once a week to discuss how to make school more meaningful for our "community" of students. We decided to go off campus once a month and take our homerooms out into the community to do a service project. We were surprised how difficult it was to find organizations willing to accommodate groups of thirty students. Some places said we could tour the location or send five or six students to work on site, but what we envisioned was actually working, getting our hands dirty. Once we found enough sites, coordinating calendars so we could all go off campus on the same dates was a nightmare. We had to leave together so we wouldn't have any coverage problems. The program was worth the trouble. At year's end, the other two seventh grade communities wanted to participate in community service.

Fortunately, Linking San Francisco and the Volunteer Center of San Francisco called us the next year to see if we needed help. They encouraged us to add a learning component to our service. Linking San Francisco was developed by the San Francisco Unified School District specifically to support service learning programs in schools. We planned monthly learning themes which we would try to teach in every academic area. When the theme was homelessness, in English class Ms. Donner and I taught such things as a poem by a homeless man. Ms. Gonzalez had her social studies students find and discuss articles in the paper on the subject. Ms. Floore and Ms. Clemenza taught their science students about homes of various animals, and in Ms. Robinson's math class, students prepared family budgets. The Volunteer Center sent us speakers on appropriate subjects. That was the good part. The bad part is we just couldn't find six service sites that could deal with thirty seventh graders all at once. The second year we did a beautiful job teaching about community issues in an interdisciplinary mode, but except for a couple of field trips by the two-strand community, service site work fell by the wayside.

At the end of that second year we got a call from a brand new organization, Partners for School Innovation. They met with us. They met with our principal, James Taylor, and checked out other programs all over the San Francisco Bay Area. They committed to give us three full-time support people. Then, thanks to Linking San Francisco, several of us were able to attend a service learning conference in the summer. We learned about evaluation and also became aware of the need to let students have more choice in their sites.

At the beginning of our third year, we started polling students as to where they would like to provide service. The majority liked the idea of working with animals or younger children. We couldn't find any animal-oriented service site that could make use of thirty students all at once. We begged, pleaded, and cajoled, but no dice. We did, at least, find six sites that could handle our numbers and work within our calendar constraints. Still, however, we didn't want to force a whole homeroom to choose a site by majority vote, so we divided each homeroom into six groups. We sent one-sixth of each homeroom along with a teacher who had interest in a site for a preliminary visit. These scout groups reported back to their originating homeroom about the pros and cons of their potential sites. All students then individually listed their first, second, and third choices for their permanent site for the remainder of the year. The seventh grade teachers then divided the students into groups based primarily on student choice, with consideration given to diversity of personalities, cultures, sexes, and abilities. This brings us back to the first service visit of the 1993-1994 school year.

Excitement bubbled as all 190 seventh grade Martin Luther King students departed in six different directions to the sites of their choice. We had service homeroom meetings each Thursday in lieu of regular homeroom to plan for upcoming site dates. In the academic classrooms, teachers organized many lessons around monthly themes (teen pregnancy and AIDS, the environment, crime, substance abuse, disabilities, homelessness, the elderly, animal protection, children's issues). Each group worked monthly at the various service locations, finding time each month to write in journals. Students evaluated their impressions of the site, how they felt helpful, what impeded their progress, what they saw other students do that was beneficial, and anything else they thought we should know. These monthly journals provided a real glimpse into the kind of growth and insight students gained from these site visitations.

At the end of the year, we asked students to offer suggestions for improvement next year. We will make some changes for next year: perhaps six-week themes rather than monthly, visits every three weeks rather than once a month, a few site replacements. We will build upon our successes and try to iron out glitches. Many seventh graders asked longingly if they could continue next year, stating that applying what they learn in the classroom to real life community problems makes school more interesting. Perhaps we have planted the seeds for future community involvement in these young people. Next year, the eighth grade teachers will spearhead a service program within the school. Partners in School Innovation and Linking San Francisco will expand to include more Bay Area schools. And so it goes...

If we can be of help in any way write to us at:
Seventh Grade Teachers
Dr. Martin Luther King, Jr. Academic Middle School
350 Girard Street
San Francisco, CA 94134
(415) 330-1500

Holicong and Lenape Middle Schools, Central Bucks School District, Pennsylvania. Report by Diane Galaton, Community Service Coordinator.

Several years ago when the Central Bucks School District converted their junior high schools to middle schools, a great many changes were envisioned for the "new" format, including the incorporation of students and teachers into academic teams that would have the ability to interrelate subjects in new and more effective ways. The district cited increased community involvement as one of the goals for the middle level mix.

Once the initial adjustments had taken place, the principals had the chance to evaluate their conversions and were confident about most of the changes. Two principals, Thomas Roberts of Lenape Middle School and Louis White of Holicong Middle School, identified one area where the expected change had not materialized: that was the area of community involvement. Together, they decided to pool some limited resources allocated from building block grant funds to hire a person already rooted in community involvement to develop and run a program for their students. In the spring of 1992, I came on board as the link between the schools and the community. A great deal of my adult life has been spent working with community agencies in volunteer projects.

At that time, both schools had small advisory groups of teachers and administrators to provide input and guidance for the start-up of the project. All felt that they wanted to see a type of volunteer corps developed where students were given the opportunity to work after school in community service organizations. My initial job was to contact area agencies and find opportunities that were age appropriate and available to students after school. After contacting 39 area agencies, 15 organizations committed to the program with experiences including child care, library work, aquatic aides, and nursing homes.

The program was introduced enthusiastically in both schools with informational flyers, announcements, and posters used to attract students' attention. However, by the final sign-up day, only 8 students from Holicong and 25 from Lenape had applied to participate – not an outstanding showing from schools with populations of over 500 students each. After doing some follow-up interviewing and coordinating schedules of students and agencies, 20 students between the two schools were placed, with signed contracts and parental approval.

Once on location, several students had excellent experiences, took their commitments seriously, and were considered beneficial by the agencies. Unfortunately, these students tended to be those that were already successful academically and socially. Not all of the students took their commitments seriously or were happy with their agency. A few just stopped showing up.

At the end of the program we sent questionnaires to the organizations and all student participants. We also asked for some comments from nonparticipants. Responses made it clear that many students at this age lacked the self-confidence to handle these types of assignments or felt uncomfortable being the only young person on site. Students also felt they could be more involved in a program that took on a specific project or dealt with a specific problem.

Clearly, we needed to rethink our approach and plan a new way to involve our students in meaningful and engaging service activities.

About the time we were scratching our heads and trying to regroup, we discovered that the state of Pennsylvania had some money available to schools that were venturing into service learning. Grants were being made available through the Pennsylvania Governor's Office on Citizen Service. Our advisory group thought that we might try developing a project using one interdisciplinary academic team per school, the idea being that we would find one agency with which the entire team could work. So, during the summer and early fall, I was given the mission of developing a grant application as well as trying to develop possible linkages and projects with community organizations.

Writing that grant proved to be an important step in formalizing the program. It helped us put into words exactly what we were trying to accomplish, how it was going to be approached, what we thought it would cost, and who was going to be involved both in the school and in the community. Getting the grant meant greater flexibility for the program and less time spent scrambling for money or supplies.

At Holicong, it was agreed that a seventh grade team would partner with A Woman's Place, the shelter for abused women and their children located in our area of the community. The team of approximately 110 students was divided into six advisory groups supervised by one teacher. My job included meeting with the teachers to launch projects, acting as liaison between school and agency, procuring supplies, tracking finances, and following up on all paperwork and meetings specified by the grant.

The project started with a visit by Susan Hauser, community education director of A Woman's Place. The team learned about violence in our society and, more specifically, domestic violence as it relates to the mission of the shelter. Students then returned to their advisories to discuss their experiences and map out their involvement. The students had decided they would conduct a drive for goods and services needed by shelter residents and that they would adopt at least one room in the shelter, being responsible for painting it, replacing curtains, and completing any other decorating they could. As much as possible, advisory and resource times would be used for accomplishing tasks.

The first part of the project began with a letter-writing campaign to over 50 local and national businesses. Students worked in pairs to compose their letters about the project and what types of goods they were seeking. Many boxes of goods were received, including cleaning supplies, bedding, canned food, and gift certificates. We also learned that legislation was about to be introduced dealing with stalking and allocation of funds for victims of domestic violence. That prompted another round of letter writing.

Meanwhile, logistics for our refurbishing had to be worked out, including supplies, participants, and travel arrangements. Over one third of the team volunteered to work on painting days, even though the initial dates planned were weekends. Eventually, we ended up taking 12 students, one teacher, and me for two days of concentrated work. The local paper featured a story on their efforts and asked some of the kids about their experiences. Students Shannon O'Malley and Douglas Brown spoke for the students, expressing their initial disbelief that this type of problem even existed in our area, but saying that they felt very good about being able to help. Students who were not able to go to the shelter to paint also organized an Easter project, making and filling Easter baskets for the children residents.

At the same time, Lenape began a project with an eighth grade team of over 100 students. Their project focused on cleaning up and beautifying two parks in the borough of Doylestown. In this project all students left the school grounds to work for one full day trimming trees, planting flowers, conditioning soil, and creating a new hiking trail.

Year one of our team-based projects was a success; enthusiasm was infectious. In year two we expanded the program to include more teams, more students, and more agencies. This did not mean everyone was thrilled, however. There was still plenty of concern about the "learning" component in these projects, the wisdom of trying to add one more thing to an already jammed curriculum, the advisability of upsetting normal scheduling, and the cost and mechanics of involving so many more students.

School year 1993-1994, however, found us off and running with seven projects between the two middle schools, after a summer that found me pursuing numerous area agencies with ideas for possible projects, some received enthusiastically and others shot down at varying stages of negotiations. (Note that this job does not fit within the confines of the "normal" school academic schedule or day.) Our goal for this year was to strengthen the ties to the curriculum so that service related more closely to what was going on in the classroom.

A super example of this was a project undertaken at Lenape by a ninth grade English/social studies team. I had been approached by a local women's group about involving some students in a centennial fair that they were planning as a celebration the group's 100th year. They were hoping a few students could come up with and run some games or activities that might have been common at a Victorian fair. This meshed perfectly with the period of American history and literature the ninth graders would be working on during the spring. As part of their study, the 54 students researched and organized all the games and activities at the Victorian fair, bringing them to life with costuming, music, equipment, and atmosphere. The local paper and the Philadelphia paper both carried stories on the fair, highlighting such activities developed and executed by the students as female boxing, hoop rolling, story telling, cakewalk, and barbershop singing. In a letter of thanks, Jeanette Dare, of the Village Improvement Association, wrote, "We stand in awe of these students' talents and abilities" and "Lenape Middle School went to great lengths to give the community a day it will long remember."

Meanwhile our seventh graders continued and expanded the successful link with the shelter for abused women and their children. Students expressed concern for the children at the shelter, so the focus of our efforts was shifted toward meeting their needs. As before, we started with an awareness program featuring agency personnel and talks in advisories about possible projects. As part of the English curriculum, students wrote children's story books. These became the basis for a regular story and play hour at the shelter. Approximately every other week, I accompanied four or five students to the shelter, where they read their stories and took part in some activity such as potato printing or clay sculpture. We also played Santa at Christmas, making ornaments and decorations, procuring a tree, and fulfilling wish lists for the children at the shelter. We wanted to make sure Santa made their dreams come true even if they were not at home.

Other teams that year took on intergenerational activities with a local senior adult day care facility, made soup for a food bank, worked on raising funds and awareness for the reconstruction of a local landmark, and worked in parks. In all, over 500 students had been actively involved in service learning activities. Grant funding had helped to pay transportation costs, buy supplies and consumables, fund training, and provide the opportunity to take a number of students and teachers to conferences. Additional funding, supplies, and services had also come from the district, the borough of Doylestown, the Village Improvement Association, parent groups, and local businesses.

As the program expands, we face a number of obstacles including finding enough cooperating agencies, dealing with the increased number of students involved, and being attentive to the concerns of parents and administration. I am encouraged by the interest the district has shown in expanding service learning throughout the district and at all educational levels. It's a constant challenge, but one that has potentially limitless rewards.

For further information contact:
Diane Galaton
59 Pine Mill Circle, Doylestown, PA 18901
(215) 345-1661

Shoreham-Wading River Middle School, Long Island, New York. Report by Joanne Urgese.

The community service program at the Shoreham-Wading River Middle School (now named the Albert G. Prodell Middle School) began modestly in 1973 when a teacher, with the help of a parent, took a few disenfranchised students to a day care center and a nursing home to work for an hour or two weekly. The program was so successful that the following year a teacher assistant was hired to expand the program. The program continued to grow as the teachers, administrators, and community members saw the benefits that service learning afforded middle school students.

Today every student is involved in at least one service unit. Over their three years in the middle school, most have had two or three experiences. What began as a pull-out program became an integral part of the classroom. A teacher coordinator and teacher assistants run the school-wide program, in addition to expanded career units and a cultural awareness program. Mini buses are driven by the staff to transport students to and from the many sites used each year. The busses are also used for career exploration trips, exchanges, district-wide field trips, and by coaches for some after-school athletic programs. This requires special licenses, yearly physicals, and safety tests for the staff members but is less expensive than renting both busses and drivers for all these trips.

Teachers choose to have their classes participate in a community service unit, and each year almost all teachers do so. Generally, a service unit is six to ten weeks in length. This includes one preparation period weekly, plus one on-site double period weekly.

Many students work with physically or mentally challenged students at both public and private schools and at a local hospital. Other students work with the elderly in adult homes, health care facilities, a veterans home, or senior day care centers. Some work with students in elementary schools, Head Start programs, and in the local public library.

Prior to beginning programs each year, the coordinator meets with each teacher, schedules all of the units for the year, and notes the type of experience the teacher would like the class to have: working with the elderly, the physically or mentally challenged, or younger kids. One month prior to each unit, sites are confirmed, speakers are booked for an orientation, and any classroom reading, writing, or video materials are readied. Permission slips, with an explanation of the unit, are prepared and sent home to the parents.

A good orientation is crucial to a successful unit. Two weeks before the first visit, a speaker comes from the site to discuss the site and population and to answer any questions students might have. (Most sites are delighted to send someone. When this is not a possibility, the community service staff does the site orientation.) A video may also be shown at this time. (All sixth grade classes see a video taken of previous programs, and seventh and eighth graders may see a video about the particular population they will be working with.) Students receive their first journal writing assignment after the orientation. In this entry, students write about their expectations. Through the orientation and journal writing, any questions or concerns are addressed in advance.

One week prior to the initial visits, students have their first preparation period and then one preparation period each week. During this time, students plan and prepare activities they will do on site. The type of activities depends upon the particular unit the teacher has chosen. For example, students may design a board game involving historical events to play with senior citizens, or they may prepare a craft to work on while they talk to their assigned person, or they may plan a sing-along, learning old songs which many of them have never heard before. When working with young children they may prepare a story hour format, picking out and practicing age appropriate books, preparing a finger play or felt board-illustrated story, and preparing a coordinating craft. Another type of unit might involve planning and preparing science, math, or social studies lessons.

In addition to the weekly preparation period, the class uses one double period weekly for the on-site visit. Students spend approximately forty-five minutes on site. The rest of the time is needed for travel.

The first visit usually includes a tour of the facility, finding out what the rules are at the site, and getting to know the people or person they will be working with. The students bring something to share or do a short lesson.

The weekly lessons require planning and preparation that sometimes take more time than the one preparation period allows. Students must finish all work as homework in these cases. For example, if the students are making paper bag puppets to go along with books to be read to nursery school students, they must pre-cut all the pieces and have a sample made. They will practice reading their books and be able to lead a finger play or felt board activity. Students who are not well prepared will struggle on site and perhaps disappoint the children who are counting on them. For this reason, students are seldom unprepared the first time and are almost never unprepared a second time. Scrambling to get work together on site and letting someone else down are two terrific incentives for being prepared.

After each visit, the students have journal writing assignments that are due the next day. They write about what transpired, what went well, what didn't go well, what could be done differently the next time, what the people they worked with were like, how they reacted towards the students, and how they felt about the experience. They are encouraged to be open and honest in their writings. The adult who was with them on site reads their journals and responds. The same adult plans with the student weekly and returns the journal to the student at that time. While students are preparing for the following trip, the group can discuss the last trip together.

Taking three periods from regular classroom activities weekly for six to ten weeks certainly is a commitment to service learning. Do the learnings justify such a commitment, and why do teachers choose to involve their students? The most obvious reason is that students learn to care about others. Over and over again the caring can be seen. Teachers see the entire spectrum of personalities within the classroom being thoughtful and helpful on site. In addition, it is obvious that students understand and learn more about people who differ from themselves. Some other objectives, which may be less obvious at first, are also realized. Students learn to plan, organize, and realize a purpose. At an age when it is critically important that students gain more self-esteem, some students who don't excel academically or socially in the regular classroom find themselves experiencing great success with service learning. On the other hand, students who never had to put forth much effort to succeed in class often find themselves having to work harder.

Academic content is reinforced when students take math or science material they have studied and teach it to others. History comes alive when students hear about the Great Depression or World War II from a senior citizen. Writing about the experience, composing letters, making a pop-up book, or reading to younger children certainly enhances language arts learning. Learnings in music, art, and physical education can be similarly improved.

In addition to the six to ten week programs, special programs occur during the year, such as a Thanksgiving food drive, music group visits to various sites, city and diverse population exchanges, groups visiting the school, and designing and implementing environmental or recycling projects.

As the program grew over the years, few obstacles were encountered, because the growth was in response to the positive benefits seen by both the school and community. It should be noted that the district was fortunate enough to have a large tax base that is now disappearing. This could prove to be a problem in future years. Sometimes a parent has had difficulty seeing the value in learning outside the classroom, but once the program is thoroughly explained, the problem usually disappears. On a few occations, a student has expressed nervousness to a parent at the beginning of the program, and the parent has shown concern. After discussing the long-range goals, the student usually continues with the project. Going to a site more than once or twice allows the student time to grow out of his/her fear of the unknown, and finally to understand and genuinely care about the population he or she is working with. Many journal entries near the conclusion of a unit state "I don't want community service to end!"

Except for an occasional problem, the very exciting experiences make everyone involved in the program say, "This is why I believe in the program so much!" Here are some examples:

- watching an eighth grade boy animatedly reading a book to a group of first graders who are gathered at his feet listening in rapt attention;

- watching a quiet seventh grader being brought out by an eighty-five year old blind woman (the woman is talking about what school was like when she was young while making a picture from interestingly shaped shells the student gathered);

- watching a student, who initially expressed fear about working with the elderly, as a tear rolls down her cheek while saying good-bye to her new friend (she promises to stay in touch, and then does);

- hearing a classroom bully gently explain to a four year old why it is wrong to hit his friend;

- watching a group of students push wheel chair-bound veterans in a conga line with the veterans grinning from ear to ear;

- and seeing the smile come across a student's face when he is warmly greeted on his second visit by a mentally challenged student.

In the initial contact with a site, it is important to explain the program fully, answer any questions, and agree on what the students can do. When communication is good there will be no difficulty using a site again. Each September, many sites call to ask when the students are coming. The students are always prepared, and an adult from the school is always with them. Our sites look forward to the students' return.

People from different sites have commented on the various needs our students fill. They care for the handicapped and fill their desire to be a part of the community and bring happiness into the lives of senior citizens. In many cases their visits are one thing the elderly look forward to each week. Teachers in both the nursery and the elementary schools have often stated that they don't know who gains more, the middle school student or the younger student.

The program is evaluated by observing the students at work, listening to both the students and the people they work with, and studying journal entries. These methods reveal that multidimensional growth is taking place. Expectations are explained to the students prior to beginning the unit. Ratings of *excellent, good, satisfactory, poor,* or *unsatisfactory* are given for their preparation, work on site, and bus behavior. No mark or test, however, can truly show the benefits service experiences will have on students throughout their lives.

Teachers recognize the positive impact that these experiences have on students' self-esteem and on their desire to do their jobs well. Working with others in the community has the same effect on the middle school teachers.

In order for any program to be effective, the school and the community must be committed to it. Fortunately, in the Shoreham-Wading River district the commitment has been strong, enabling all middle school students to participate and grow through service to others.

One student's journal entry provides a fitting summary. "I really don't like community service. I love it! It's much more interesting than sitting in a classroom all day. It's better getting out and getting a real life experience. I think community service is a great learning experience in that you deal with other people and how they act and feel and are. I also think community service is more of a preparation for the real world than classwork could ever give you."

For further information contact:
    Albert G. Prodell Middle School
    Randall Road
    Shoreham, New York 11786
    (516) 821-8266

Mansfeld Middle School, Tucson, Arizona. Report by Cheri Bludau.

Many schools in the Tucson Unified School District (TUSD) have implemented some form of community service. The main format used is a community service day during which students of an entire school or grade level spend time serving the community. Some schools also offer community service classes. TUSD has a Community Partnership Department that oversees many community service programs. Generally, teachers are the coordinators of any service programs offered.

The district has developed, in cooperation with the business and industrial sectors and post secondary institutions, a Partners-In-Education Program entitled, "The Fourth R: All Children Will Graduate Prepared For the World of Work." A specific goal of the "Fourth R" is to prepare all students for responsible and participatory citizenship. To quote from our goals, "Schools access all available community-based service agencies to enhance the educational opportunities available to students." District personnel were excited about the opportunities offered to some middle schools to infuse service learning into the curriculum. This offered the district a means of fulfilling another component of their "Fourth R." – that "students recognize the relevance of what they learn and be able to apply their knowledge to on-the-job and real life experiences."

In 1993, the Social Science Education Consortium at the University of Colorado in Boulder invited a team of teachers from TUSD to participate in a National Science Foundation grant project, "Enhancing the Middle School Curriculum Through Community Service." While at the institution, four teachers and one administrator created a model unit dealing with world hunger called, "The Kids' Guide to Hunger." The four teachers each work at a separate school, and therefore the model unit has been implemented in a variety of ways. However, "The Kids Guide to Hunger" integrates science, social studies, and community service in each school. The amount of time needed for the unit varies (two to nine weeks or even an entire year).

Mansfeld Middle School was one of the sites that had a teacher attend the institute. A seventh grade team of six teachers representing language arts, math, science, social studies, physical education, and career technology chose to adapt "The Kids' Guide to Hunger" model to reflect an integrated thematic unit. One hundred and thirty students were involved directly with the study. However, the entire faculty, staff, and student body participated in some component of the study and service. Small businesses located close to the school as well as the people at the community food bank were both helpers and recipients of the services.

The students had identified world hunger as a priority concern for our society. If the students themselves had not identified hunger as a major concern, the unit would probably have to change; for students must have a real interest in the topic in order for the service component to come to life.

To begin the studies we completed several activities. The students filled in KWL Charts (charts noting what the students *know*, *what* they would like to learn, and what they did *learn*). Following the KWL feedback, the students attended a hunger meal, at which 15% of the students receive a full meal of hamburgers, french fries, and chocolate milk; 25% of the students receive a tortilla, refried beans, and water; and 60 % receive rice and water. Needless to say, as the food was served, murmurs of disapproval could be heard. An example of the numerous emotional exchanges will demonstrate the learning that occurred at the meal. One student states, "All I have is rice. I want to move over there where they have better food." A teacher replied, "Do you think there are people in this world that feel the same about moving to another county – maybe the United States?" Afterward the students wrote their reflections on the meal. It was interesting to note that the students with the rice used stronger strokes in the formation of their letters and many exclamation marks. Some even punched holes in their papers! Most of the students having hamburgers felt embarrassed about their plenty and wanted to share. There were a few who just gloated over their good fortune. The meal brought home the inequality of world food supplies in such a strong way for the students that it impacted many of their future decisions on how to help the community. The meal also created an awareness of the difficulty in tackling such a mammoth problem – how can we solve the world's food problem? The students soon came to the conclusion that they first needed to work on their own local community to begin to solve this problem.

What happened next was an intensive period of service with the food bank tied directly to what the students were studying. The school had never donated more than one hundred cans of food during the periodic food drives, so the students decided that education for all the students of Mansfeld about the local hunger problem was needed. They developed a two week course of study for the school population while implementing a super food drive. The students devised a variety of activities ranging from economic studies (including cost of living versus minimum wage math lessons) to population studies and interviews with people at the Food Plus Bank. All numbers used in the economic lessons were authentic for the Tucson community. The video class filmed and produced a very moving tape of the Food Plus program to share with the school. The result of this effort was that Mansfeld Middle School collected over 1000 cans of food! The students organizing the food drive did not want to offer rewards for the class with the most cans. They felt people should give because they know the food is needed. They did relent and offered an early lunch pass to any class that met its goal, but incredibly, most of the students at Mansfeld were more interested in whether the goal of one thousand cans could be broken than whether they got the lunch pass! The drive was so successful that this year the student council is using many of the same strategies for the holiday food drive.

Another service activity involved having students develop "square foot gardens." The goal was to grow the gardens and then distribute the resulting plants at the food bank. The students felt just giving cans of food was not the answer to the local hunger problem, but only a temporary solution. They wanted to teach people to grow some of their food, and specifically food indigenous of the Tucson desert land. A side benefit of establishing square foot gardens was a solution to another problem the students identified as a serious issue – trash! By using the garbage from our school, composted through worms, the students made fertilizer to add to the soil. The students ran out of time in growing the plants, mainly because of the time needed to build the boxes, but they did make some fertilizer.

This year's team decided to pick up where the previous team left off, but they also decided to change the goal slightly. They are presently working at the local botanical gardens apprenticing composting. They will select several methods of composting the school's trash, including last year's worms. Instead of building square foot gardens, the students are seeking a garden area space at the local Native American reservation to grow a community garden. Since students from the reservation attend Mansfeld, this service activity will be a collaboration of the middle school, the elementary feeder school on the reservation, and the people of the reservation. We hope the students can encourage families from the community to develop a plot at the garden area.

The major obstacles we faced in adapting "The Kids' Guide to Hunger" were time and transportation. Scheduling speakers, service activities, and special events was difficult with six teachers, one hundred and thirty students, parents, and the number of individuals involved with each activity, not to mention just the length of time it takes to complete some of the activities. One solution to some problems is to have mini-service activities that students volunteer to engage in after school and/or on weekends. These are quite successful. We limit the number of students in order to have more effective interaction and are able to develop more expertise with the smaller groups of students. We have also continued some total group service activities. Transporting our students continues to be a challenge. Usually we either walk or ride school buses to the service activities. We are presently seeking a school van to transport children to the mini-service activities.

For further information contact:
Mansfeld Middle School
1300 E. Sixth Street
Tucson, Arizona 85706
(520) 617-6120

Mansfeld Middle School
Tucson Unified School District
Service Learning Component

MISSION STATEMENT

Student service learning is the integration into the curriculum of youth service with an emphasis on academic learning.

GOALS

1. Builds critical thinking skills.
2. Enhances academic performance.
3. Fosters relevant engaged learning.
4. Promotes active citizenship.
5. Improves self-esteem and self-concept.
6. Develops a service ethic.
7. Teaches leadership skills.
8. Increases sense of social responsibility.
9. Provides career exploration.

OBJECTIVES

1. To show that students can make a difference.
2. To present students with a menu of options from which to choose their service activities.
3. To enable students to focus on one agency and channel their service activities.
4. To foster cooperation and group dynamics and develop a collaborative effort among students.

KIDS' GUIDE TO HUNGER

Lesson One: Sources of Food
OBJECTIVES

1. Assess students' knowledge on hunger and food.

2. Explain how all of our food comes directly or indirectly from plants.

3. Formulate a definition for the process of photosynthesis.

4. Identify, chart, analyze, and discuss food sources in the six geographical regions.

5. Demonstrate the contributions of early Native American cultures and their food.

ACTIVITIES

1. KWL Chart (What do you know? What do you want to know? What did you learn?): Obj. #1

2. A Poverty, Hunger, and Overpopulation Scavenger Hunt: Obj. #1

3. Search for Starch (Lab/2 parts): Obj. #2 and Obj. #3

4. Visit a store or restaurant and find out where they get their food: Obj. #2

5. Main Foods of the World Map/Reading: "Staple Foods"/ Staple Foods Lesson: Obj. #4

6. Charting Main Foods of the World/Thought Sheet/Chart Master: Obj. #4

7. Native Americans and Our Diet: Obj. #5

8. Amazing Maize: Obj. #5

Evergreen School, Hillsboro, Oregon. Report by Ethel Graham, Principal.

Evergreen School is a 7-8-9 middle school in a suburban/rural area near Portland. There are about 900 students and 50 staff members in our building. Evergreen's service learning program, Respecting All Others, was developed in conjunction with our character education program. The goal behind the service component is to develop community awareness in students, help students learn the value of giving to others, and create bonds between different cultures, age groups, and interest groups in the community. Over 500 students are involved each year, which is well over half our student population. Senior citizens who volunteer in the school are involved, as well as nearly all staff members and many parent volunteers.

Service at Evergreen has evolved to include a great deal of student planning and "voice." The projects are different each year, depending upon student interest. They must fall under one of three categories: intergenerational service, service to the minority community, and environmental service. These categories come under a broad umbrella and are easily tied to the curriculum, both in character education and in the areas of social studies, science, and health. Since Evergreen is a school with a great deal of teaming and integration of curriculum, integrating service across the curriculum at each grade level is a natural.

One value of service is that students have begun to see their community in a different way, and they see that they are responsible, as young citizens, for helping to make a difference. They help to feed and clothe needy families in our attendance area. They work with the elderly in care centers to provide these people with some outside contact and companionship. They support local environmental causes by building bird houses and bat boxes, providing stream and beach cleanup, and "nature-scaping" the school grounds with native plants that require little care once they are established. They teach younger children about Oregon's 21st Century Schools Act and help them to develop portfolios

of work. They write stories for young readers and then print and bind the books.

It is easy to see how such projects can tie in to the more traditional school curriculum. In science, particularly at grade seven, environmental studies are tied to studies of biomes, cycles, and earth science. Evergreen School is adjacent to a small wetlands area and there is a larger, regional wetlands project in our community, so the opportunities for meaningful environmental service abound.

Intergenerational service and service to the minority community tie in with health objectives as students study families and aging. Culture studies in social studies, economics, immigration, and current events are easy to relate to student-generated service projects.

Evergreen has just completed the final year of a three-year service learning grant. Service to the school and community is now an expected part of each student's experience at Evergreen. While there is not 100 percent student participation, the number is growing each year. This is because staff members are increasingly comfortable with suggesting, supervising, and evaluating service projects and because the community is more aware of what students are able to offer.

The only obstacles to instituting service learning in our school were lack of experience and lack of funding to get us started. The lack of funding was solved by a Serve Oregon grant, which was available as flow-through federal money. Funding gave us some teacher release time to plan our work and the money for materials, busses, and trips to service sites. Once funding was available, teachers were willing to give much time and energy to developing beginning projects. Since service is contagious and self-sustaining, once we began to work on projects, kids, teachers, and community members were able to generate lots of ideas for further work. When momentum builds for service, doors open in the community and all other obstacles are swept away.

Although no previous school-wide culture existed for service, there were some programs in existence through the National Junior Honor Society and other clubs that used service as a way for students to belong. Service is now firmly entrenched as part of our school culture and part of our curriculum, with each team designing a service component for at least one unit throughout the year.

Active service programs can generate community funding though other grant dollars. The school district will offer in-kind support to keep service going, because it generates good will in the community and positive stories in the local papers. Teachers will give of their time, because they see how service reaches all learners, especially students traditionally defined as "at-risk" who may have had little opportunity to give something of themselves to others.

There are so many wonderful service learning stories in our building that it is hard to choose some to highlight. Since Evergreen teaching teams regularly utilize interdisciplinary and integrated curriculum, it is also difficult to describe exactly which goals of the curriculum area are met through service learning. In an art class, the design and execution of a mural are easily related to course goals. The following examples of service learning projects are related to social studies and to our character education program, which emphasizes understanding of other cultures and service to the community.

One seventh grade team developed service projects to complement their "Community in Unity" unit. The unit focused upon cultural likeness and differences in our own community, the concepts of communities in science, and physical and mental health issues in our community. Students identified needs, particularly in our growing population of migrant farm workers. The students built on a program begun last year to collect clothing, and wash, repair, and display it attractively in a room called The Closet. Families and students were invited to visit The Closet to select the clothing they need in a private setting. The clothing was appropriate for middle schoolers, so kids felt good about getting it.

As part of the same unit, another group of students collected food donations for the Thanksgiving meal at Centro Cultural, a nearby agency providing services to the migrant community. They also decorated the dining hall and helped with dinner preparations. Food baskets were put together to deliver to Evergreen families in need, and the entire school worked together to make the baskets last at least through the month of December.

When one of the food baskets was delivered, the teacher and counselor discovered one family in dire need of additional services, including medical attention. The staff and students rallied to collect money for medical bills, arrange support services from the community, and provide ongoing assistance for the family during the remainder of the school year.

This is a good example of how service learning is self-sustaining and how it can capture the imagination of staff members and students. Students certainly developed insight into the needs of a large, often unseen, segment of our community. They learned about cooperation, generosity, and gratitude. They identified the need in our community for more health services for the poor. And they recognized that they could influence adults to join them in making a difference in our community.

Another ongoing service learning project involves the Wetlands Project. This work is tied directly to goals in life science, particularly in the area of biomes, communities, and cycles. Students are working to maintain and restore habitats both in the small wetlands adjacent to our building and in the larger Jackson Bottom Wetlands. They study the wetlands biome, learn about the interdependence of the wildlife and habitat, and then spend time improving the wetlands through clean-up of banks, restoration of native plants, building of bat and bird boxes, and study of wildlife patterns. The work on this project will continue to be part of the seventh grade team curriculum for the foreseeable future.

Students are learning more than social studies and science. They are using service as a vehicle for authentic learning experiences that enrich the concepts learned in their classrooms and make those concepts come alive. They can see a real-life application for their skills and are constructing their own learning from the work they do.

Intergenerational service at Evergreen has been defined as service to those both younger and older than the students. Student groups have developed projects working with both age groups.

Students on the eighth grade Superstars team developed a project with the help of our community liaison. They identified a residential assisted living facility where the senior citizens would welcome a relationship with a youngster of middle school age. They learned a bit about each resident. Then they designed and assembled Christmas stocking door hangers personalized with the residents' names. They included small gifts, large-print crossword puzzles, and other interesting things and delivered them personally, taking the time to visit with "their" senior citizen and learn about that person's life and interests. This service was related to the students' social studies curriculum, in which they were studying family systems and community.

Another intergenerational project involved younger children. In language arts class students studied elements of children's literature. They wrote and illustrated simple children's stories and bound them into books. They then traveled to a nearby elementary school, read the stories to first and second graders, and donated the books to the library. They enjoyed the experience of sharing their work with younger students, and their writing was more meaningful because it was done for a genuine audience.

A final example of service to the community with the specialty subjects that is directly tied to the curriculum is this year's Advanced Art mural project. Students in the Advanced Art class were invited by the local library to design the entrance to the children's section. Since this branch library may move soon, the entrance design would have been in the building for only a few years. As students began to work on the project, they included students from Technology II, the advanced building class at grade nine. The builders built a framework for the entrance that can be moved when the library moves. The artists worked in groups to come up with a design. They submitted four master designs to the library board. When one was selected, the entire class worked for two months to transfer the elaborate design, paint it, and seal it. The panels were delivered to the library by students and adult volunteers and were installed. There was a wonderful dedication ceremony, complete with a ribbon-cutting by the mayor. The kids felt great to know that their work will be on the entrance to the children's library now and when they move the library as well.

In our school, service learning is loosely overseen by the school site council. They are the body that approves management of all grant funds. As service receives more funding from the general fund, it is likely that teams will report service activities directly to the assistant principal in charge of curriculum.

Evaluation is done on a project-by-project basis. Students are usually asked to write a reflective piece on their learning to include in their portfolio. There are items in the annual student, parents, and staff survey that relate to service as well. Further evaluation of the quality and value of service projects is needed and will be developed this year.

As Evergreen approaches a new school year, the staff and students are excited about expanding the opportunities for service to all students. We are committed to the principle that community service enriches those who give far more than those who receive. We have seen it work magic for students as they learn that they are capable of making a tangible contribution to the community. We will not go back to less active, less productive ways of learning, but will move forward with the integration of service-based learning across the curriculum.

For further information contact:
Evergreen School
550 N.E. Evergreen Road
Hillsboro, Oregon 97124
(503) 640-8900 Δ

9 Service Learning Resources

The ultimate goal of middle level education is the development of capable students who have the skills needed to acquire knowledge, who can utilize that knowledge in real life situations, who have the ability to identify and solve problems, and who are beginning to understand themselves and their place in society. We believe that service learning is an important component in establishing an effective middle level program committed to these goals.

Throughout this book we have provided information designed first to help you understand the value of creating a culture of service in your school and second to direct your thinking about ways to start this process. This chapter provides additional resources in three specific areas. First, it provides information on resources that will help you understand effective middle level practices. Middle schools with successful guidance programs, a team organization, and active parent and community involvement are more likely to have successful service learning programs. Second, it provides additional references related to service learning at the school and classroom level. Finally, it lists organizations and agencies that can provide still further information and technical support for those establishing service learning programs.

Books

Middle School

Ames, N.L. & Miller, E. (1994). *Changing middle schools: How to make schools work for young adolescents.* San Francisco: Jossey-Bass.

This book tells the story of four urban middle level schools involved in major school reform efforts. Noteworthy chapters focus on teaming showing what is possible when a team works together and on recommendations for enhancing school reform.

Beane, J. (1993). *A middle school curriculum: From rhetoric to reality.* Columbus, OH: National Middle School Association.

This critical and widely acclaimed work presents the concept of an integrated curriculum based on the interests and needs of students. It includes a reasoned and a detailed proposal as well as a critique of the separate subject approach.

Carnegie Council on Adolescent Development. (1989). *Turning points: Preparing American youth for the 21st century.* New York: Carnegie Corporation.

This is a seminal and influential work that describes the critical importance of effective middle level education. It presents recommendations for developing a program that best serves the young adolescent learner, which includes connecting schools with communities, implementing interdisciplinary teaming, and reengaging families in the education of young adolescents.

Carnegie Council on Adolescent Development. (1995). *Great transitions: Preparing adolescents for a new century.* New York: Carnegie Corporation.

This book highlights the needs of adolescents as they enter the 21st century. It focuses on re-engaging families, educating and promoting the health of adolescents, strengthening the community, and addressing the power of the media.

Hawkins, M.L. & Graham, M.D. (1994). *Curriculum architecture: Creating a place of our own.* Columbus, OH: National Middle School Association.

Refreshing, candid, and challenging, this publication advances the notion that each school must create its own curriculum based on local needs and realities, with real student involvement.

Irvin, J.L. (1992). *Transforming middle level education: Perspectives and possibilities.* Needham Heights, MA: Allyn and Bacon.

This text contains twenty chapters by leading experts in middle level education. Of particular usefulness to those interested in service learning are Chapters 3 and 4, which discuss the characteristics of middle level learners; Chapter 5, which addresses home, school, and community connections; and Chapter 9, which provides insight to the role of the team in socializing students.

Lounsbury, J.H. (Ed.). (1992). *Connecting the curriculum through interdisciplinary instruction.* Columbus, OH: National Middle School Association.

This book is a functional resource that provides information on nearly every phase of interdisciplinary instruction – research, planning, examples, and evaluation processes.

Meinbach, A.M., Rothlein, L., & Fredericks, A.D. (1995). *The complete guide to thematic units: Creating the integrated curriculum.* Norwood, MA: Christopher-Gordon Publishers.

This publication provides a rationale for the development of interdisciplinary units and a step-by-step approach to the design and implementation of specific units. Topics covered include: development of thematic units, assessment, and parent and community involvement in the curriculum.

National Association of Secondary School Principals, Council on Middle Level Education. (1985). *An agenda for excellence at the middle level.* Reston, VA: Author.

This is a brief but powerful paper wherein the twelve dimensions of schooling necessary for excellence at the middle level are examined.

National Association of Secondary School Principals, Council on Middle Level Education (1988). *Achieving excellence through the middle level curriculum.* Reston, VA: Author.

The fifth and final volume in the series that began with *An agenda for excellence*, this paper is designed to assist administrators and staff in capturing their vision and their reality.

National Middle School Association. (1995). *This we believe: Developmentally responsive middle level schools*. Columbus, OH: Author.

A re-visioning or reconceptualization of the ideas and ideals of middle level education is presented in this landmark position paper. Following a rationale, twelve characteristics of developmentally responsive middle level schools are described.

Service Learning

Andrus, Elaine (1995). Service learning and middle school students: The perfect fit. In Y. Siu-Runyan & V. Faircloth (Eds.), *Beyond separate subjects: Integrative learning at the middle level*. Norwood: MA. Christopher-Gordon.

A nationally recognized expert provides a good overview of service learning and relates it to contemporary reform efforts.

Bolin, F.S. (1990). *Growing up caring*. New York: Glencoe/McGraw Hill Education Division.

This textbook for students was designed to help them clarify their values and make decisions regarding caring for themselves, others, their family, and the community.

Conrad, D., & Hedin, D. (1987). *Youth service: A guidebook for developing and operating effective programs*. Washington, DC: Independent Sector.

This manuscript makes recommendations for developing the specific components of a service learning program. It provides materials that are useful for a service learning coordinator.

Council of Chief State School Officers. (1994). *The service learning planning and resource guide*. Washington, DC: Author.

Lists of federal, state, and local agencies involved with service activities.

Duckenfield, M. & Swanson, L. (1992). *Service learning: Meeting the needs of youth at risk.* Clemson, SC: The National Dropout Prevention Center.

This manuscript gives a concise presentation of service learning opportunities for at-risk youth.

Fertman, C.I. (1994). *Service learning for all students.* Bloomington, IN: Phi Delta Kappa.

This manuscript identifies the four basic elements of effective service learning programs. It outlines a step-by-step process for implementation and provides specific examples of various types of programs.

Goldsmith, S. (1995). *Journal reflection: A resource guide for community service leaders and educators engaged in service learning.* Washington, DC: The American Alliance for Rights & Responsibilities.

This manuscript contains information and recommendations for a wide range of journal practices and activities to help ensure that journal reflection in service learning really does assist in the development of thoughtful, responsible people.

Henderson, K. (1990). *What would we do without you? A guide to volunteer activities for kids.* Crozet, VA: Shoe Tree Press.

This manuscript identifies specific examples of the ways teens can make a difference in their community. It shows how to identify a community need and develop appropriate student-centered activities.

Maryland State Department of Education (1995). *Maryland's best practices: An improvement guide for school-based service learning.* Baltimore: Author.

This document is the product of interviews with 80 teachers who use service learning as a teaching method. The best practices for service learning are presented, along with potential pitfalls.

Salzman, R., & Reisgies, T. (1991). *150 ways teens can make a difference: A handbook for action.* Princeton, NJ: Peterson's Guides.

The handbook includes ideas for service activities in several social issue areas and lists organizations students can contact for information on volunteer opportunities.

Stephens, L.S. (1995). *The complete guide to learning through community service grades K-9.* Boston: Simon and Schuster Company.

This is a hands-on guide to implementing service learning. It includes over 400 activities that are organized either by subject or interdisciplinary theme. The activities are drawn from actual teaching experiences.

Curriculum Development and Materials

Service Learning

Active citizenship today: A handbook for middle school teachers by the Close Up Foundation, 44 Canal Center Plaza, Alexandria, VA 22134. Phone: 703-706-3640.

The handbook features interactive lessons and tips on implementing service learning in both the classroom and community.

Active citizenship today: Field guide, making it happen by the Close Up Foundation, 44 Canal Center Plaza, Alexandria, VA 22134. Phone: 703-706-3640.

This guide offers students a practical resource for tackling community problems.

Adventures of adolescents by Catherine A. Rolzinski (1990). Youth Service America, 1319 F St., N.W., Suite 900, Washington, DC 20004.

This manuscript explores the experiences of seven middle school youth service programs.

Changing our world: A handbook for young activists by Paul Fleisher (1993). Zephyr Press, P.O. Box 13448, Tuscon, Arizona 85732-3448.

A guidebook and practical manual that will help young advocates and potential advocates develop the knowledge and skills needed to give them confidence in the belief that they can make a difference.

Curriculum integration, coordinator roles, and collaborations: Evaluation of the Pennsylvania 1994-1995 Learn and Serve Grant Program by C. Fertman, J. Long, L. White, Y. Yugar, J. Miller, and J. Ross (1995).

This report highlights service learning progress in Pennsylvania.

Cultivate positive cultural behaviors through caring and outstanding citizenship program by the Colorado Service-Learning Resource Center, Colorado Department of Education, 201 E Colfax Avenue, Denver, CO 80203. Phone: 303-866-6897.

This pamphlet describes the Q.U.E.S.T. program, an alternative education program offered at Euclid Middle School in Littleton, Colorado, for 7th graders of all ability levels.

Design, leadership and models: The change agents of school service learning programs by Harry Silcox (1994). Brighton Press, Inc., 64 Lempa Rd., Holland, PA 18966.

This book provides model program descriptions and strategies to use in the development of service learning programs.

Draft instructional framework in service learning for middle schools by the Maryland Student Service Alliance, 200 W. Baltimore St., Baltimore, MD 21201. Phone: 410-767-0358.

This curriculum guide provides unit plans for service learning projects that center around four issues: poverty, aging, environment, and peer tutoring/club projects, tied into science, social studies, math, English/language arts, and vocational education classes.

Effective service learning:Creating a culture of service for middle, junior, and senior high students by I. Buchen, and C.I. Fertman (1994). For more detailed information call 1-800-448-2197.

This ESL curriculum links learning with community service. Six sets of 35 student workbooks each contain eight experientially-based sessions and exercises.

Enriching the curriculum through service learning by Carol Kinsley and Kate McPherson (1995). Association for Supervision and Curriculum Development, 1250 N. Pitt Street, Alexandria, VA 22314-1453, Phone: 703-549-9110.

This is a practical guide to service learning. It describes service learning projects that have enhanced the curriculum in schools across the nation and that have improved student learning in the process.

Growing hope: A sourcebook on integrating service into the school curriculum, edited by Rich Willits Cairn and Jim Kielsmeier (1991). National Youth Leadership Council, 1910 West County Rd. B, Roseville, MN 55113. Phone: 612-631-3672.

This sourcebook offers background, definitions, rationale, nuts-and bolts implementation, sample program materials, and resource materials.

Growing together: An effective advisory program by the Colorado Service-Learning Resource Center, Colorado Department of Education, 201 E Colfax Avenue, Denver, CO 80203. Phone: 303-866-6897.

This manuscript explains the advisory program for 6th, 7th, and 8th graders at Whittier Middle School in Norman, OK. The daily program includes reading, intramurals, guidance, discussion, projects, and activities.

Joining hands: Community service learning resource kit reviewed and revised by Dr. Rahima Wade (1995). The University of Iowa, Service Learning Department, 215 Seashore Hall Ctr., Iowa City, IA 52242-1402.

This kit contains community service learning ideas and a list of reference materials and agencies to contact regarding specific service learning topics. This information and more provides quality, organized outlines for implementing successful service learning projects.

The kid's guide to service projects by Barbara A. Lewis (1995). Free Spirit Publishing, 400 First Avenue N., Suite 616, Minneapolis, MN 55401-1724. Phone: 1-800-735-7323.

This book contains more than 500 ideas for service for young people of all ages. The projects range from simple things kids can do on their own to large-scale commitments that involve whole communities.

Kid's guide to social action by Barbara A. Lewis (1991). Free Spirit Publishing, 400 First Avenue N, Suite 616, Minneapolis, MN 55401-1724. Phone: 1-800-735-7323.

This is a classroom guide for solving social problems and turning creative thinking into positive action.

Learning by giving. K-8 Service Learning Curriculum Guide (April 1993). National Youth Leadership Council, 1910 West County Rd. B, Roseville, MN 55113.

This curriculum guide is filled with lesson plans and resource materials for integrating service into the curriculum.

Learning by serving: 2,000 ideas for service learning projects by Joseph Follman, James Watkins, and Dianne Wilkes (1994). SouthEastern Regional Vision for Education (SERVE) affiliated with the School of Education, University of North Carolina at Greensboro.

This "idea book" is for people interested in initiating or expanding service learning in their schools and communities. It has an excellent service learning resource section and bibliography.

National youth service: Answer the call. A resource guide (1994). Youth Service America 1101 15th Street, N.W., Suite 200, Washington, DC 2005. Phone: 202-296-2992, Fax: 202-296-4030.

This resource guide is a tool for youth and national service practitioners, educators, other youth workers, youth policy makers, parents, and young people who are interested in knowing more about national and community service.

No kidding around! America's young activists are changing our world and you can too by Wendy Schaetzel Lesko (1992). Information USA Inc., P.O. Box E, Kensington, MD 20895 Phone: 301-942-6303.

This handbook on civic activism contains strategies for launching a campaign and over 1,000 resources to aid in developing concrete proposals for social, legal, and political change.

Routes to reform: Service learning K-8 curriculum ideas written by teachers from Generator Schools, a National Service Learning Initiative Project (1994). National Youth Leadership Council, 1910 West County Rd. B, Roseville, MN 55113. Phone: 612-631-3672.

This book contains more than 50 descriptions of effective service learning projects, grades K-8.

Service learning in the middle school curriculum: A resource book (1995). Social Science Education Consortium, P.O. Box 21270, Boulder, CO 80308-4270.

This resource book is designed as a useful starting place in teachers' efforts to integrate service learning with the middle school curriculum.

Service learning reflections: Update of service learning in Pennsylvania by C. Fertman, I. Buchen, J. Long, L. White (1994).

This report highlights service learning programs throughout the state of Pennsylvania.

Sharing success in the Southeast: Promising service learning programs by James Watkins and Dianne Wilkes (1993). SouthEastern Regional Vision for Education (SERVE) affiliated with the School of Education, University of North Carolina at Greensboro.

This publication highlights over 30 effective service learning programs in the Southeast.

Skills for adolescence (6-8) (1995). To order, call Quest International, 537 Jones Rd., P.O. Box 566, Granville, OH 43023-0566. Phone: 1-800-446-2700.

This Lions-Quest curriculum specifically helps teachers reinforce and enrich critical assets of young people's lives through comprehensive classroom curricula focusing on life skills, active citizenship, and service to others. To use it you must attend a three-day workshop near your city.

Standing tall teaching guide, grades 6-8 (1992). The Giraffe Project, P.O. Box 759, Langley, WA 98620. Phone: 206-321-0757.

Activities that can be used by a classroom or club that teaches the steps of powerful social action. It includes stories of "giraffes," people who stick their necks out to help the community.

Teens, crime, and the community by the National Crime Prevention Council and the National Institute for Citizen Education in the Law, Washington, D.C.

This guide comes in two versions: a guide for students and a guide for teachers. The junior and senior high school curriculum inspires students to take active roles in crime prevention. It addresses teen victimization, victim assistance, violence, the criminal justice system, property crime and vandalism, child abuse, date rape, and other issues.

Teacher training manual by the Maryland Student Service Alliance, 200 W. Baltimore St., Baltimore, MD 21201. Phone: 410-767-0358.

A practical guide for the educator, this manual gives the basics of service learning and infusion and provides guidance for challenges such as transportation, funding, press coverage, and liability.

Things that work in community service learning (1995). For list and prices, contact the Community Service Learning Center, 333 Bridge St., Springfield, MA 01103. Phone: 413-734-6857. Fax: 413-747-5368.

This is a series of monographs describing successful middle school experiences in every content area. They are written by teachers and are based on real curriculum units.

The training toolbox: A guide to service learning training by the Maryland Student Service Alliance, 200 W. Baltimore St., Baltimore, MD 21201. Phone 410-767-0358.

This manual contains six different agendas that can be used to train teachers, administrators, parent groups, and community-based organizations to be effective champions of service learning.

VYTAL (Volunteer Youth Training and Leadership) (1993). The manual is available from VYTAL, c/o Greater Pittsburgh Camp Fire

Council, 730 River Ave., Suite 531, Pittsburgh, PA 15212. Phone: 412-231-6004.

This is a comprehensive collection of activities that enable students to see the value of service and to develop specific action plans.

What you can do for your country (January, 1993). Report of a commission of the National and Community Service Coalition, 409 3rd Street, SW, Suite 200, Washington, DC 20024. Phone: 202-488-7378.

This report summarizes the current state of community service in the country after the first year of the commission's formation.

Whole learning through service: A guide for integrating service, K-8 (1990). Order this guide from The Community Service Learning Center, 333 Bridge St., Springfield, MA 01103. Phone: 413-734-6857. Fax: 413-747-5368.

This curriculum provides teachers with community service learning experiences that can be used to generate learning in content areas.

Youth service: A guidebook for developing and operating effective programs by Dan Conrad and Diane Hedin. Published by the Independent Sector, 1828 L. Street, NW, Washington, DC 20036. Phone: 202-273-8100.

This guidebook provides assistance to people wishing to begin, expand, or promote programs of youth community service. It features current information on youth community services and practical, down-to-earth advice for designing, organizing, running, promoting, and supporting youth service programs.

Reflection

A how-to guide to reflection by Harry Silcox (1993). Brighton Press Inc., 64 Lempa Rd., Holland, PA 18966.

This book explores the service learning movement and the use of reflective teaching as a critical component in blending experience with school curricula.

Learning helpers: A guide to training and reflection by the National Center for Service Learning in Early Adolescence, CASE/CUNY, 25 W. 43rd St., Suite 612, New York, NY 10036-8099. Phone: 212-642-2946.

This guide provides reflection and training tools appropriate for young adolescents who serve with children ages 2-10.

Learning through service (1989). Project Service Leadership, 12703 N.W. 20th Avenue, Vancouver, WA 98685. Phone: 206-576-5070. Fax: 206-576-7068.

This guide helps teachers and community advisors more effectively facilitate discussions and reflective activities.

Reflection: The key to service learning (1991). National Center for Service Learning in Early Adolescence, CASE/CUNY, 25 W. 43rd St., Suite 612, New York, NY 10036-8099. Phone: 212-642-2946.

This book outlines the ways reflection may be used to transform a community service project into a quality learning experience. It includes rationale, sample activities, and steps for integrating reflection into service learning program.

Special Populations

Something shining like gold ... but better (1991). National Youth Leadership Council, 1910 West County Rd. B, Roseville, MN 55113. Phone: 612-631-3672.

This is a manual for the National Indian Youth Leadership Program's nationally successful, intensive leadership program for Indian youth.

Special education service learning guide (1995). Maryland Student Service Alliance, Maryland State Department of Education, 200 West Baltimore St., Baltimore, MD 21201. Phone: 410-767-0358.

This newly revised guide provides adapted plans for service learning projects in the areas of aging, poverty, environment, literacy, substance abuse, bias, and the school. It also provides introductory skill activities and guidance for adapting projects and procedures for students with various kinds of disabilities.

Liability

Benefits & labor issues under the national and community service act (1993) by Charles Tremper and Anna Seidman. Published by the Non Profit Risk Management Center, 1001 Connecticut Avenue, N.W., Suite 900, Washington, DC 20036.

No surprises: Controlling risks in volunteer programs, by Charles Tremper and Gwynee Kostin (1993). Non Profit Risk Management Center, 1001 Connecticut Avenue, N.W., Suite 900, Washington, DC 20036.

Videos

Citizen stories (1991). Close Up Foundation, 44 Canal Plaza, Alexandria, VA 22314. Phone: 1-800-765-3131.

The video focuses on five individuals of varying ages and backgrounds who opted for action over apathy. The accompanying guide includes activities to lead students to ponder the meaning and varied aspects of social responsibility.

The courage to care: The strength to serve (1994). Maryland Student Service Alliance, Maryland State Department of Education, 200 West Baltimore St., Baltimore, MD 21201. Phone: 410-767-0358.

This is a service learning motivational video that explains what service is and shows students participating in service learning projects.

Hearts and minds engaged (1994). West Publishing Company, School Division D4-13, 620 Opperman Dr., P.O. Box 64779, St. Paul, MN 55164-0779. Phone: 612-687-7482. Has an accompanying text: *Community service learning guide*.

Shows examples of middle and high school service learning programs in Washington State.

Routes to reform: Service learning &school improvement (1994). National Youth Leadership Council, 1910 West County Rd. B, Roseville, MN 55113. Phone: 612-631-3672.

This video takes a close look at three exemplary programs in elementary, middle, and senior high schools across the United States.

Service learning: Transforming education (1995). Linking San Francisco, SFUSD, Parkside Center, Room 22; 2550-25th Avenue; San Francisco, CA 94116 Phone: 415-759-2882.

This video profiles three K-12 service learning projects in San Francisco public schools.

Organizations Active In Service Learning

Corporation for National Service
1201 New York Avenue, NW
Washington, D.C. 20525
Phone: 202-606-5000; Fax: 202-565-2794

Created by the 1993 National and Community Service Trust Act, the Corporation has a responsibility for administering and distributing federal funds directly and in partnership with state commissions. Principal parts of the Corporation's work are the AmeriCorps national service program, the National Senior Volunteer Corps, and Learn and Serve America. Learn and Serve America incorporates school-based programs that create service learning initiatives for young people in K-12 and higher education.

National Association of Partners in Education, Inc.
901 N. Pitt Street, Suite 320
Alexandria, Va 22314
Phone: 703-836-4880; Fax: 703-836-6941

The National Association of Partners in Education, Inc. (NAPE) is the only national membership organization devoted solely to the mission of providing leadership in the formation and growth of effective partnerships that ensure success for all students. NAPE defines "partnership in education" as a collaborative effort between a school(s) or school district(s) and one or more community organizations with the purpose of improving the academic and personal growth of America's youth." Through the IDEALS Project, NAPE utilizes its model process for developing partnerships to support the integration of service learning in the subject-matter curricula of schools, an approach differing markedly from many community service programs that offer or require after-school activities or a single class addressing public service issues. The IDEALS' service learning pilot sites include a high school and elementary school in Washington, D.C. and Calvert County's (MD) middle schools where there is district-wide integration across all subject matter.

National Service-Learning Cooperative. The K-12 Learn and Serve America Clearinghouse

This organization is sponsored by the National Youth Leadership Council and the University of Minnesota College of Education, and is funded by the Corporation for National Service.

The National Service-Learning Cooperative provides leadership, knowledge, and technical assistance to support and sustain service-learning program areas within six primary audiences: Learn and Serve America grantees and sub-grantees, K-12 teachers and administrators, community-based organizations, colleges and universities, state and local officials, and the general public. It offers a toll-free information number, national database of programs and resources, a library of materials, an electronic bulletin board, referrals to training, peer consultants, and other resources, and operates regional technical assistance centers.

Information on its Clearinghouse and Cooperative Partners is listed on the next two pages.

The Cooperative Partners

The Clearinghouse
University of Minnesota
Vocational & Technical Ed. Bldg.
1954 Buford Ave., R-290
St. Paul, MN 55108
Phone: 1-800-808-SERVE (7378)
     (612) 625-6276
e-mail: serve@maroon.tc.umn.edu

National Technical
Assistance Center
National Youth Leadership Council
1910 West Country Road B
St. Paul, MN 55113-1337
Phone: (612) 631-3672
e-mail:NYLCUSA@aol.com

National Specialists
Close Up Foundation
44 Canal Center Plaza
Alexandria, VA 22314
Phone: 703-706-3640
e-mail: cufmail@ix.netcom.com

National Indian Youth Leadership
Project
P.O. Box 2140
Gallup, NM 87301
Phone: (505) 722-9176
Fax: (595) 722-9794
e-mail: machall@prevline.health.org

Regional Information Centers
Youth Service California
Haas Center for Public Service
Stanford University
558 Salva Tierra Walkway
Stanford, CA 94305-8620
Phone: (415) 723-3803
Fax: (415) 725-7339
e-mail:cr.mas@Forsythe.stanford.edu

University of Massachusetts
Teacher Education Department
School of Education, Furcolo Hall
Amherst, MA 01003
Phone: (413) 545-1339 or 545-4727
Fax: (413) 545-2879
e-mail: cslric@acad.umass.edu

Regional Technical
Assistance Centers
Arkansas Department of Education
4 State Capitol Mall, Room 405 B
Little Rock, AR 72201
Phone: (501) 682-4399
Fax: (501) 682-4618

Community Service-Learning Center
333 Bridge St., Suite 8
Springfield, MA 01103
Phone: (413) 734-6857
Fax: (413) 747-5368
e-mail: ckinsley@K12.oit.umass.edu

Constitutional Rights Foundation
601 South Kingsley Drive
Los Angeles, CA 90005
Phone: (213) 487-5590
Fax: (213) 386-0459
e-mail:crfcitizen@aol.com

Project Service Leadership
12703 NW 20th Avenue
Vancouver, WA 98685
Phone: (360)-576-5070
Fax:(206)-576-5068
e-mail: Mcphers@pacifier.com

National Dropout Prevention
Center*
Clemson University
205 Martin Street
Box 345111
Clemson, SC 29634-5111
Phone: (864)656-2599
Fax: (803) 656-0136
e-mail: mbdck@prism.clemson.edu
*also Regional Information Center

East Bay Conservation Corps
1021 Third Street
Oakland, CA 94607
Phone: (510) 891-3900
Fax: (510) 272-9001
e-mail: ebcc-rlm@holonet.net

Michigan K-12 Service-
Learning Center
Michigan State University
Suite 253 Erikson Hall
East Lansing, MI 48824-1022
Phone: (517) 432-2940
Fax: (517) 355-4502
e-mail: raudenbl@pilot.msu.edu

PA Institute for Environmental and
Community Service Learning
Philadelphia College of
Textiles & Science
Henry Ave. and Schoolhouse Lane
Philadelphia, PA 19144
Phone: (215) 951-0343
Fax: (215) 951-0345
e-mail: parrillolor@hardy.texcsi.edu

National Youth Leadership Council (NYLC)
1910 W. County Road B, Suite 216
Roseville, MN 55113
Phone: 612-631-3672; Fax: 612-631-2955

NYLC provides leadership training for youth and community service efforts worldwide. NYLC sponsors the National Service-Learning Cooperative/Clearinghouse.

Council of Chief State School Officers
One Massachusetts Avenue, N.W.,#700
Washington, D.C. 20001-1431
Middle-grade school/state policy initiative
Phone: 202-335-7029
Community service learning initiatives
Phone: 202-408-5505; Fax: 202-408-8072

The Council of Chief State School Officers is the only national education organization composed of superintendents and state commissioners of education. Through legislation and publications, the Council has supported K-12 service learning for the past eight years. In addition, the Council advocates for funding of service learning programs and works to link service learning to school reform and school-to-work opportunities.

National Helpers' Network, Inc.
245 Fifth Avenue, Suite 1705
New York, NY 10016-8728
Phone: 212-679-2482; Fax: 212-679-7461

The National Helpers' Network is an independent nonprofit organization that carries on the work formerly performed by the National Center for Service-Learning in Early Adolescence. It helps develop model service learning programs known as "Helper Programs," operates a clearinghouse for practitioners, advocates, and policy-makers concerned with education reform and meeting the needs of young ado-

lescents, and provides field training through its central staff and network of field associates.

Educational Commission of the States (ECS)
707-17th Street, Suite 2700
Denver, Colorado 80202-3427
Phone: 303-299-3611; Fax: 303-296-8332

ECS is a national organization created to help state political education leaders improve the quality of education. The objective of ECS is to create new operating and policy environments that support flexibility, accountability, and responsiveness in public education and that will result in improved student achievement at all levels, both K-12 and post-secondary. ECS joined with NYLC to convene this forum of service learning, school reform, and higher education, and has planned further meetings to continue the dialogue.

Accelerated Schools Project
Ceras 109, Stanford University
Stanford, CA 94305-3084
Phone: 415-725-3095; Fax: 415-723-7578

This project is a comprehensive approach to school change designed to improve schooling for children in at-risk situations. Accelerated schools provide challenging learning environments traditionally reserved for gifted students to all students in elementary school, and the project is expanding into middle and high school. Through the National Center, training and ongoing assistance is provided to the approximately 700 accelerated school communities in 37 states.

American Association of School Administrators
Total Quality Management Schools
1801 North Moore Street
Arlington, VA 22209
Phone: 703-875-0766; Fax: 703-841-1543

AASA is a professional organization for nearly 17,000 educational leaders across the United States and Canada and in many other parts of the world. Its mission is to support and assist these and other education leaders to achieve the highest quality education. AASA advocates for improving the condition of children, maintaining and strengthening essential leadership skills, preparing schools for the challenges of the 21st century.

Association for Supervision and Curriculum Development (ASCD)
1250 N. Pitt Street
Alexandria, VA 22314-1453
Phone: 703-549-9110; Fax: 703-549-3891
ASCD is community of educators committed to creating opportunities in teaching and learning for the success of all learners. Recently ASCD published a useful handbook entitled, *How to Establish a High School Service Learning Program* by Judith T. Witmer and Carolyn S. Anderson, with step-by-step practical advice on program development.

Coalition of Essential Schools and Institute for School Reform at Brown University
1 Davol Square
Providence, RI 02903
Phone: 401-863-3384; Fax: 401-863-2045

The Institute for School Reform focuses on the "fault line" between theory and practice in America's schools. The mission of the Institute is to provoke, support, nurture, understand, and track reform efforts, in part through the Coalition for Essential Schools. This coalition identifies and documents the work of schools engaged in promising academic practices, including service-learning. The Institute is administering a $150 million grant from Walter Annenberg designated to directly support reform at the school and teacher level.

High Success Network
Transformational Outcome-Based Education
P.O. Box 1630
Eagle, CO 81631
Phone: 970-328-1688; Fax: 970-524-9820

The High Success Network is a consulting organization that provides direct assistance to state, intermediate, and local districts interested in the rationale, strategic design, implementation, and documentation of Transformational Outcome-Based Education (TOBE). It sponsors and conducts national and regional conferences relating to TOBE. They focus on helping school districts and their communities create a view of the future that includes service learning.

Campus Compact
c/o Brown University, Box 1975
Providence, RI 02912
Phone: 401-863-1119; Fax: 401-863-3779

Campus Compact is a national coalition of 500 college and university presidents who believe that institutions of higher education have a primary responsibility to foster students' sense of civic responsibility and to contribute to the welfare of their communities. Campus Compact also runs the Project on Integrating Service and Academic Study to support and expand the role of faculty in service initiatives.

Additional Organizations

National Institute for Work and Learning
1200 18th Street, N.W.,Suite 316
Washington, DC 20036
(202) 887-6800

National Society for Experiential Education (NSEE)
3509 Haworth Drive, Suite 207
Raleigh, NC 27609-7229
(919) 787-3263
Fax: (919) 787-3381

National Alliance for Youth Development
148 S. Victory Blvd.
Burbank, CA 91502
(818) 848-1993

Youth Service America
1101 15th Street, N.W.,Suite 200
Washington, DC 20005
(202) 296-2992

Generations United
440 1st Street, N.W.,Suite 310
Washington, DC 20001-2085
(202) 638-2952

Independent Sector
1828 L. Street, N.W.
Washington, DC 20036
(202) 273-8100

Alliance for Service Learning in Education Reform
One Massachusetts Avenue,N.W.
Suite 700
Washington, DC 20001-1431
(202) 336-7026

Institute for Responsive Education
605 Commonwealth Avenue
Boston, MA 02215
(617) 353-3309

Center for Human Resources
Brandeis University
60 Turner Street
Waltham, MA 02154
(617) 489-2487
Fax: (617) 489-2487

Search Institute
700 South Third Street, Suite 210
Minneapolis, MN 55415
(612) 376-8955
Fax: (612) 376-8956

Service Learning Evaluation Network
University of Pittsburgh
5D21 Forbes Quad
Pittsburgh, PA 15260
(412) 648 7196
Fax: (412) 648-7198

National and Community Service
Coalition
409 3rd Street, S.W., Suite 200
Washington, DC 20024
(202) 488-SERV (7378)
FAX: (202) 488-1004

Foundations

**DeWitt Wallace-Reader's
Digest Fund**
23rd Floor, 2 Park Avenue
New York, NY 10016
(212) 251-9720
Contact: Andy Fisher

Points of Light Foundation
1737 H Street, N.W.
Washington, DC 20006
(202) 223-9186

William T. Grant Foundation
515 Madison Avenue, 6th Floor
New York, NY 10022
Phone: (212) 752-0071
Fax: (212) 752-1398

W.K. Kellogg Foundation
One Michigan Avenue East
Battle Creek, MI 49017-4058
(616) 969-2680
Fax: (616) 969-2693

Funding

The Federal Register
Superintendent of Documents
U. S. Government Printing Office
Washington, DC 20402-9325
Phone: 202-512-2465

The Foundation Center
79 Fifth Avenue
New York, NY 10003-3076
800-424-9836
Fax: 212-620-4230

The Grantsmanship Center
1125 W. Sixth Street, Fifth Floor
PO Box 17220
Los Angeles, CA 90017
213-482-9860
Fax: 213-482-9863

Liability

**Association Insurance
Management**
216 S. Peyton St.
Alexandria, VA 22314-2813
800-468-4200

**Non Profit Risk Management
Center**
1001 Connecticut Avenue, NW
Washington, DC 20036

References

Anderson, C.S. and Witmer, J.T. (1994, Fall) Addressing School Board and Administrative Concerns about Service Learning. *Democracy & Education,* 33-37.

ASLER (1993). *Alliance for service-learning in education reform - Standards for school-based service-learning.* Washington, DC: Author.

Barber, B. (1994)." Citizenship Education" presentation, "Citizenship Education: Mandating Service at the State Level" conference, Maryland.

Beane, J. (1992). Letting go. Visions of the middle school curriculum. In P. George, C. Stevenson, J. Thomason, & J. Beane, *The middle school and beyond* (pp. 81-103). Alexandria, VA: Association for Supervision and Curriculum Development.

Beane, J. (1993). *A middle school curriculum: From rhetoric to reality.* (2nd ed.). Columbus, OH: National Middle School Association.

Bloom, J. (1952). *Educational taxonomy.* New York: Harper.

Boyer, E. (1983). *High school: A report on secondary education in America.* New York: Harper and Row.

Boy Scouts of America (1994). *Guide to safe scouting: A unit leader's guide for current policies and procedures for safe activities.* Irving, TX: Author.

Buchen, I. and Fertman, C. (1994). *Creating a culture of service: Effective service-learning.* Warminster, PA: Marco Products.

Carnegie Corporation. (1989). *Turning points. Preparing American youth for the 21st century.* New York: Carnegie Corporation.

Carnegie Corporation. (1992). *A matter of time.* New York: Author.

Conrad, D. and Hedin, D. (1989) *High school community service: A review of research and programs.* Madison, WI: National Center on Effective Secondary Schools.

Dewey, J. (1916). *Democracy and education*. New York: Macmillan.

Erikson, E. H. (1980). Youth and the life cycle. In R. E. Muuss (Ed.). *Adolescent behavior and society: A book of readings* (3rd ed., pp. 226-237). New York: Random House.

Fertman, C. I. (1994). *Service learning*. Bloomington, IN: Phi Delta Kappa Educational Foundation.

Fertman, C. I. (1993). Creating successful collaborations between schools and community agencies. *Children Today* 22(2):32-34.

Fertman, C. I. (1993). *Service star reports*. Pittsburgh, PA: University of Pittsburgh.

Fertman, C. I., Buchen, I., Long, J., and White, L. (1994). *Service-learning reflections: Update of service-learning in Pennsylvania*. Pittsburgh, PA: University of Pittsburgh.

Fertman, C. I., Buchen, I., and Long, J. (1993). *The Pennsylvania serve-America grant: Implementation and impact, year 1*. Pittsburgh, PA: University of Pittsburgh.

George, P. S., and Alexander, W. M. (1993). *The exemplary middle school* (2nd ed.). New York: Harcourt Brace Jovanovich.

Havighurst, R. J. (1972). *Developmental tasks and education*. New York: McKay.

Honnet, B.P., and Poulson, C.P. (1989). *Service-learning standards*. New York: National Society for Internships and Experiential Education.

Huberman A.M., and Miles, M.B. (1984). *Innovation up close: How school improvement works*. New York: Plenum Press.

Jacobs, H.H. (1989). *Interdisciplinary curriculum: Design and implementation*. Alexandria, VA: ASCD.

Juhasz, A. M. (1982). Youth, identity, and values: Erikson's historical perspective. *Adolescence, 18*(67): 443-450.

Kane, M.B., and Khattri, N., (September 1995). Assessment reform: A work in progress. *Phi Delta Kappan, 77* (1), 30-32.

Kendall, J. C., and Associates. (1990). *Combining service and learning: A resource book for community and public service*, (Vols. I and II). Raleigh, NC: National Society for Internships and Experiential Education.

Kilpatrick, W. H. (1940). *Group education for a democracy.* New York: Association Press.

Kinsley, C.W. and McPherson, K. (1995). *Service learning.* Alexandia, Virgina: Association for Supervision and Curriculum Development.

Kohlberg, L., and Hersh, R. H. (1977). Moral development: A review of the theory. *Theory into practice, 16*(2), 53-59.

Kurth, B. (September, 1995). Learning through using service learning as the foundation for a middle school advisory program. *Middle School Journal, 27*,(1), 35-41.

Menge, C. P. (1982). Dream and reality: Constructive change partners. *Adolescence, 17*(66), 419-442.

Muuss, R. E. (1980). Identity in adolescence. In J. Adelson (Ed.). *Handbook of adolescent psychology.* New York: Wiley.

National Association of Secondary School Principals (1985). *An agenda for excellence at the middle level.* Reston, VA: Author.

National Middle School Association (1995). *This we believe: Developmentally responsive middle level schools.* Columbus, OH: Author.

Newmann, F. M. (1989) Reflective Civic Participation. *Social education, 53*(6), 357-359.

Secretary's Commission on Achieving Necessary Skills (S.C.A.N.S.) (1994). *Teaching the S.C.A.N.S. competencies.* Washington,DC: U.S. Department of Labor.

Smith, D.W., Redican, K.L., and Olsen, L.K. (1992). The longevity of growing healthy: An analysis of the eight originial sites implementing the school health curriculum project. *Journal of School Health, 62*(3), 83-87.

Thornburg, H. (1983). Is early adolescence really a stage of development? *Theory into Practice, 22*, 79-84.

Toole, P. and Toole, J. (1995). Reflection as a tool for turning service experiences into learning experiences. In C. Kinsley and K. McPherson (Eds.) *Service learning*. Alexandia, Virgina: Association for Supervision and Curriculum Development.

U.S. Department of Education, (1993). *America 2000: An educational strategy sourcebook*. Washington, DC. Author.

U.S. Department of Education, (1991). *Collaboration to build competence: The urban superintendents' perspective*. Washington, DC. Author.

W.T. Grant Foundation. Commission on Work, Family and Citizenship (1988). *The forgotten half: non college youth in America; an interim report on the school-to-work transition*. Washington, DC: Author.

Woo, I. (1995). Creek restoration for environmental elementary kids. Bryant Elementary School. Seattle School District.

About the Authors

Carl I. Fertman, Assistant Professor and Director of the Maximizing Adolescent Potential Program, School of Education, University of Pittsburgh, is the founder and director of the Pennsylvania Service Learning Evaluation Network. Dr. Fertman has authored a number of books, reports, and articles on service learning and has also written about school and community agency collaboration to promote student health and academic success.

George P. White, Associate Professor and Program Coordinator of Educational Leadership, Lehigh, University, Bethlehem, Pennsylvania, is the founder and director of the university's Middle Level Partnership. This consortium is dedicated to the study of education systems designed to meet the needs of the pre-adolescent leader. Dr. White is a member of NMSA's Family and Community Advocacy Committee.

Louis J. White is a retired administrator in the Central Bucks School District in Doylestown, Pennsylvania. He continues active as a consultant on middle level topics for the Lehigh University Middle Level Partnership and as a site visitor for the Pennsylvania Service Learning and Evaluation Network.

The authors recognize with appreciation the special contributions of the staff and students of the Central Bucks School District, Doylestown, Pennsylvania, where our work with service learning began.

NATIONAL MIDDLE SCHOOL ASSOCIATION

National Middle School Association, established in 1973, is the voice for professionals and others interested in the education and well-being of young adolescents. The association has grown rapidly and enrolls members in all 50 states, the Canadian provinces, and 42 other nations. In addition, 57 state, regional, and provincial middle school associations are official affiliates of NMSA.

NMSA is the only association dedicated exclusively to the education, development, and growth of young adolescents. Membership is open to all. While middle level teachers and administrators make up the bulk of the membership, central office personnel, college and university faculty, state department officials, other professionals, parents, and lay citizens are members and active in supporting our single mission – improving the educational experiences of 10-15 year olds. This open and diverse membership is a particular strength of NMSA's.

The association publishes *Middle School Journal*, the movement's premier professional journal; *Research in Middle Level Education Online; Middle Ground, the Magazine of Middle Level Education; Target*, the association's newsletter; *The Family Connection*, a newsletter for families; *Classroom Connections,* a practical quarterly resource; and a series of research summaries.

A leading publisher of professional books and monographs in the field of middle level education, NMSA provides resources both for understanding and advancing various aspects of the middle school concept and for assisting classroom teachers in planning for instruction. More than 70 NMSA publications are available through the resource catalog as well as selected titles published by other organizations.

The association's highly acclaimed annual conference, which has drawn approximately 10,000 registrants in recent years, is held in the fall. NMSA also sponsors an annual urban education conference and a number of weekend workshops and institutes.

For information about NMSA and its many services, contact the association's headquarters office at 4151 Executive Parkway, Suite 300, Westerville, Ohio, 43081. TELEPHONE: 800-528-NMSA; FAX: 614-895-4750; INTERNET: www. nmsa.org.